Looking for Oliver

Looking for Oliver

A Mother's Search for the Son She Gave Up for Adoption

Marianne Hancock

Jessica Kingsley Publishers
London and New York

First published in the United Kingdom in 2003
by Jessica Kingsley Publishers Ltd
116 Pentonville Road
London N1 9JB, England
and
29 West 35th Street, 10th fl.
New York, NY 10001-2299

www.jkp.com

Copyright © 2003 Marianne Hancock

Library of Congress Cataloging in Publication Data

Hancock, Marianne, 1948–
  Looking for Oliver : a mother's search for the son she gave up for adoption / Marianne Hancock.
    p. cm.
  ISBN 1-84310-142-4 (pbk.)
  1. Mothers and sons--Fiction. 2. Birthmothers--Fiction. 3. Adoption--Fiction. 4. Adoptees--Fiction. I. Title.

PR6108.A53L66 2003
823'.92--dc21

2002043374

British Library Cataloguing in Publication Data
A CIP catalogue record for this book is available from the British Library

ISBN 1 84310 142 4

Printed and Bound in Great Britain
by Athenaeum Press, Gateshead, Tyne and Wear

Contents

Part One

Chapter One

"That's okay," said Emma. The words were clipped. She held the phone in one hand and twisted the wet potato peeler around in the other. "I'll just have to go on my own. Anyway, see you in a bit." She placed the receiver down hard and clenched her teeth. At the other end, Michael held the dead line in his hands and shook his head despairingly. He wished he hadn't called her. It was only to say he'd be late, but he'd been bombarded with the latest run down on his mother-in-law's health and Emma's need to visit her.

In a mixture of temper and tears, Emma carried on peeling the potatoes aggressively. There was no need for either, she knew, but somehow Michael's capable and seemingly uncaring independence clashed with her highly strung character and added to her stress. She glanced up at the clock. Five o'clock. She was already craving a glass of wine.

"Hiya Mum!" Chloe breezed in bringing the cold October air in with her. She dumped her rucksack on the table and the resulting air movement caused a recent postcard from Simon to fall from the Welsh dresser onto the floor. Chloe picked it up, scanning her brother's witty travelog once again before she put it back. Then she stooped down to rub a demanding dog's ears, words tumbling as she did so. "Guess what? Mr Parker is dead pleased with my sociology piece on animals in the home. I reckon Stewart fancies me. Rob was saying he's been asking all about me."

Emma could hardly keep up with her seventeen-year-old daughter's love life, but felt uplifted by Chloe's sunny mood. She smiled at her warmly as she massaged a growing band of tension at the back of her head.

"What time's Dad coming home?" Chloe asked.

Sam, their brindle boxer, began sniffing around the kitchen floor for dropped morsels.

"About six, I hope, depending on the meeting and traffic." Emma now put the potatoes in a roasting pan together with two chicken portions under the grill. It wasn't worth cooking Chloe's soya mince until nearer serving-up time.

"How's Grandma?" Chloe asked quietly, picking up on her mum's tense mood. Emma realized that her daughter had a new ring in her nose. She thought it rather unattractive but felt disinclined to criticize or pass judgement, having herself once been a subject of dubious trends and reckless behaviour. A memory washed over Emma and she shook her head as if to toss it away. Strange, these flashbacks. You'd have thought time would have eradicated them. But no. Oh, by comparison to how Emma had been, Chloe was no problem. She was a good daughter, vivacious, but relatively sensible.

"Not too good. I think I'll have to go and visit them this weekend. I'll know better then." Emma mentally shuddered. She dreaded the drive from Cambridge to Newcastle. She'd only done the journey alone once before, all other times Michael had been with her, usually with the children, and he'd always insisted on driving, having chauvinist opinions on female drivers. Emma had never protested, not liking driving anyway.

At six o'clock on the dot, Emma heard Michael's key in the door followed by the sound of his coat being hung on the hall stand and his briefcase on the telephone table.

"Hello love. Meeting go okay?"

"I think so." He pecked her on the cheek, a habit not a demonstration of affection, his face felt cold and she caught the familiar smell of his wood musk aftershave. Then he turned to fuss Sam, who was ecstatic at his return. The fact that these emotional reunions happened every day did little to diminish the dog's euphoria. "I'm hoping we've clinched the deal with Bedford Fabrications and as long as we give them the right price with the promise of early delivery we should get it."

"Good," said Emma. At long last, Michael's engineering company seemed to be climbing out of the recession – they'd had to reduce the workforce and cut back on hours, but it now seemed that things were on the up and up. "Chloe love, would you clear the table for dinner, please?"

"Yep, just doing it. Hiya Dad. Grandma's poorly." Chloe scooped a pile of homework notes and a couple of text books and dropped them onto the spare chair.

"So what's this with your mother?" asked Michael as the three of them sat down to eat.

"Not so good. I think I ought to go and see her."

"Oh dear. You know it's impossible for me to get away from the office to take you?"

"I know that. I shall drive up myself." Emma stiffened – the tension tightened round her head. She gulped her wine. "I just need to know if you're here this weekend, for Chloe."

"I can look after myself !" protested Chloe.

"I know, love." Emma fixed her stare at Michael, "Are you?"

"Yes, yes I'm here. Why shouldn't I be?" He returned her look.

Chloe picked up a familiar undercurrent of tension. "Do you want me to come with you, Mum?"

"No, love" smiled Emma, warmed by her daughter's kindness, "No, I'll be fine. Really."

Kathleen Hargreaves sat sleeping in the armchair. Her legs were badly swollen and she had them raised on a footstool.

"What did the doctor say, Dad?" Emma asked.

Her father looked tired. Apart from rheumatism and a chesty cough in bad weather, Jack still enjoyed good enough health. It was Emma's mum who was cause for concern.

"He's prescribed another course of antibiotics and water tablets, but he says bed rest is the best thing. She has fluid on her lungs."

Emma went into their kitchen to put the kettle on. A dirty plate was on the work surface and two unwashed saucepans still on the cooker. She washed them all and left them to drain. The kitchen at 37 Boulter Street. The same yellow formica table and chairs. The same clock ticking on the mantelpiece. Next to the clock stood a photo of her brother, Steven, and his wife, now in Canada. On the other side of the clock was an old school portrait of her own children: Simon, at about ten, and Chloe when she was eight. Emma made a mental note to give them a more recent photo.

She took a couple of mugs out of the cupboard and made them both a cup of tea. It seemed weird, just her being there, without the rest of the family. It reminded her of when she was a teenager, still living at home with her parents. And of Oliver.

"Here we are, Dad," said Emma, carrying the tray of tea into the living room. Kathleen remained fast asleep. Emma was concerned as much for her father as her mother. Dad was useless without Mum looking after him. With Steven now in Canada, she was the only family member around to care for her parents. And it was about 240 miles from home in Cambridge to Newcastle. "Has Mum had anything to eat?"

"Just a drink of milk. Said she didn't fancy much else. I did myself a tin of new potatoes and mince." He sounded pleased with himself.

"I know, I've just washed your pots." Emma smiled. She got on better with him these days. "So when's the doctor calling again?"

"In the morning after surgery. You see, it's getting her to the bathroom," he lowered his voice. "...and it's not easy."

"I'm sure it's not, Dad." Emma recoiled. Goodness, she hoped neither Chloe nor Simon would ever have to take her to the toilet.

Kathleen opened her eyes. "Oh it's you, love," she enthused, stretching out a hand for Emma. "How lovely to see you, how lovely…"

Emma moved and squatted beside her mum, put an arm around her shoulder and held her hand. "How are you feeling? Do you want anything to eat? Drink?"

"No, no, I'm all right thank you, my love. How are the children?"

"They're fine, Mum."

"And Michael?"

"Fine," she said, squeezing her mum's hand softly.

On Sunday after lunch, Emma left her parents to return home. The doctor had promised to call daily until she improved. He had mentioned the possibilty of a visiting district nurse or home-help, and reassured Emma that her mother was in safe hands and would be up and about again in no time.

Emma prepared to leave, comforted, but felt the warning signs of a migraine and a rise in her stomach at the thought of the journey home. It was important she got back before dark and already it felt cold enough for a slight frost. She was terrified of driving in the dark. Emma sat in the car with the window wound down, a grey drizzle hung damply in the air.

Her dad stood in his worn slippers, a collarless shirt and braces to see her off. She thought he looked thin, old. Lost. Emma felt protective towards him. To both her parents. Not that they'd ever been a close family. He turned back indoors with a sad little wave.

"C'mon, kiddar," Emma said to herself. "Let's go."

"Simon phoned while you were at your parents," Michael sat at the kitchen table with the daily paper, eyes focused on the crossword but nevertheless aware of her fumbling in the cupboard for paracetamol. "Said he was testing the phone they've just had reconnected. I told him they'd better have an itemized phone bill."

"Too true," gulped Emma, swallowing two tablets with a glass of water, "it'll be the girls that make all the calls! Everything else okay?"

Simon was at Brighton University doing Three Dimensional Design. Chloe was doing Arts subjects at A level and fluctuated between wanting to go to university and becoming a guide dog trainer. She helped out regularly at the local veterinary practice where Emma worked part-time as a receptionist.

"He sounded as if he was enjoying life," said Michael. "I told him Grandma wasn't well and you'd gone to Newcastle. Obviously you got there and back in one piece." Michael glanced up at Emma. "How was your mother?"

Emma went to the fridge to see if there was any wine, and finding enough for two full glasses, poured one out for herself and one for Michael and sat down. She knew that wine and paracetamol were an unwise mixture but she was desperate to relax. Chloe had gone to see her friend, taking Sam, leaving the house unusually peaceful.

"She seemed old. They both did."

"I guess it happens to us all."

"Mmm." Emma sipped her wine, kicked off her shoes and closed her eyes.

Michael absorbed himself once more in the crossword, perching his half moon reading glasses on the end of his nose. They hadn't hugged or kissed since she'd returned, and now they resumed their own individual thoughts. Even with her eyes closed, she knew what he was doing, the familiar silence, peaceful but isolating, the scratch from his pencil as he filled in a clue, the habitual cough of concentration followed by a soft grunt of satisfaction. The tablets and alcohol now stilled her racing thoughts, and she gently reflected on the weekend, 37 Boulter Street, and memories.

Emma had met Michael when she'd just returned from New York feeling directionless; she had literally bumped into him at Gatwick Airport. He had just finished an engineering degree in London and was temporarily employed as a baggage handler. Immediately attracted by her long straight red hair, orange Mary Quant mini-dress and slim brown legs, he'd rushed to help carry her two large holdalls. She'd liked his confidence and charm and had given him her Newcastle address; it seemed distance was likely to prevent further contact. However, when a job interview took him to Newcastle later that year he took the opportunity to look her up. He never got the Newcastle post, but eventually secured a positon in Cambridge. They still lived in Cambridge, and now he was Company Director of his own engineering firm.

Not as slim as he used to be (but neither was she) and a bit thinner on top, her husband was still a good looking man. His thick brown hair, now greying at the temples, gave him a distinguished quality. He wore well cut suits and liked to buy clothes from Marks & Spencers. It sometimes made Emma chuckle that she was married to a man who bought clothes from Marks. Her parents, especially her mother, had been so pleased when she'd announced her engagement to Michael. Within the first year of their marriage, she'd wanted a baby so badly, Simon had been born.

A scuffle and banging in the hall shattered the peace and brought Emma back to reality. Sam barged by in a desperate rush for his water bowl near the back door as Chloe flopped onto the kitchen chair. Michael peered over his glasses at her in wry, mock disapproval.

"You made it then! How's Grandma?"

"Hello, love. Yes, I made it. Mmm, not too good." Emma felt slightly woozy.

"Poor Granddad, I bet he's really worried."

Yes, poor Granddad, thought Emma silently, closing her eyes again and drifting off into her own thoughts. He wasn't able to look after himself, let alone Mum. He went to work, she cooked the meals; both functioning in their stereotyped roles, neither communicating nor sharing.

In some ways, her own marriage had become merely a financially better off, middle class carbon copy. It had been Michael's detachment that had warmed her to him in the first place. He, in turn, had been intrigued by Emma's inaccessibility, her melancholy air of mystery. He didn't pry, he liked her that way, they respected each other's privacy.

Yet it disturbed and surprised her that Oliver seemed to be in her thoughts every day now. Just little thoughts, like wanting to know he was well, wondering if he was happy. But, of course, she would never know. And neither the children, nor even Michael, knew of his existence.

Emma now drifted in and out of sleep. She heard Michael put the kettle on as Chloe chattered amiably away, and as she listened to the soft hum of their voices, the echo of her reflections – or perhaps the wine and parecetamol – left a sense of isolated detachment within her.

Later that week Emma's father called to say Mum had taken a turn for the worse and gone into hospital. Emma replaced the receiver shakily, having arranged to go up to be with them straight away. She tried to grasp what was happening. She caught sight of her reflection in a mirror. Her short amber hair, now dulled with age and rinsed with henna, did little to soften the lines on her face. She looked tired and old. And all the worry now over her parents emphasized the lines on her own brow. She pulled a face at her image, first sucking in her cheeks in an attempt to effect slimness then pulling her jaw up with her hands. "God, I must do something with myself," she vowed silently.

When Michael arrived home, Emma was already on her second glass of wine. He sensed his wife's stress immediately and held a diplomatic silence.

"I shall drive up straight from work. There's plenty of food in the fridge so you'll just have to help yourselves." Emma sighed. "I imagine I'll be back Monday morning. All being well."

Michael offered to take her himself on Saturday but was grateful she declined on the grounds that that wasn't soon enough.

At 8.30pm Friday night, the phone rang. Michael answered, knowing it would be Emma. She had already phoned to say she'd arrived safely but had promised to call again after visiting her mother.

"Michael, it's me…"

"Hello Emma, how are things?"

"Michael, Mum's just died."

Michael drove straight up to Newcastle to be with his wife and father-in-law. Chloe had reassured him she was capable of looking after everything at home and insisted he go immediately.

Both Emma and her father were back at Boulter Street by the time Michael arrived at almost midnight. Jack sat in his familiar armchair, ashen and silent.

"Thanks for coming, Michael," said Emma.

Michael shrugged; it was the least he could do. "Are you okay?" he asked Emma quietly.

Emma nodded, but slid her eyes towards Jack.

"Can I do anything? Get anyone anything? Pop…?"

"No, no thank you," said Jack thinly. He tried to smile, but his drawn face and watery eyes were weighted with grief. "I'm fine."

Emma sighed and ran her hands through her hair. "Mum had a heart attack," she explained. "She wouldn't have known much about it – but it was so sudden. Such a shock."

To be honest, Michael was more concerned for Emma than anyone else, perhaps selfishly. He felt she was emotionally weak, quick to feel anxious and particularly bad at handling this kind of thing.

"Perhaps we'll both stay with Dad tonight – if that's okay? Do you think Chloe will be all right? What do you think, Mike?" Emma's voice sounded strained.

Michael nodded. His mind suddenly filled with work and an urgent delivery that had to be out tomorrow. "Of course," he heard himself saying. "And I'm sure Chloe will be fine."

"I can manage, really…" whispered Jack.

"No Dad, I'll stay a few days. There's things to er, sort out. Perhaps Michael might want to go back tomorrow?"

Jack looked up to meet her gaze, "I'm very grateful that you're both with me now, but you must both go back home tomorrow. I'll be all right. There's nothing I can't deal with." Jack seemed to mean it. "You've done more than enough for me. I'd prefer to be on my own. Really."

Michael knew Jack meant it when he said he wanted to be alone. He was a solitary man who often resented company – even his daughter's. Although they got on much better now than they used to.

Michael phoned Chloe to tell her they were staying with granddad that night and although it was nearly 1am, was comforted with Chloe's alert and reassuring independence. Yes, she would keep the doors locked. Yes, she would feed the dog. No, he wasn't to worry and she'd expect to see them whenever – no hurry. Look after Granddad.

It was three in the afternoon when both Michael and Emma arrived back home in convoy. Chloe burst into tears as soon as she heard the key in the door. She threw herself over the dog for comfort but Sam squirmed away in protest.

"Oh no! Poor Granddad – what will he do without Grandma?"

"I don't know." Michael didn't want Emma to be forever driving up and down spending weekends visiting her father. As it was, she was in the bathroom being sick. He knew he was being inconsiderate, but when Emma got stressed out – everyone suffered. Himself in particular. His mind flashed back to when the children were small, especially when Simon had been born, her postnatal depression, some strange obsession that she might lose him, recurrent nightmares of him being snatched away, the migraines… What was it she'd taken for years? Librium, or something. He shuddered at the memory.

"Are you ready?" asked Michael impatiently. He was standing by the open living room door, car keys dangling in his hands. They had a table booked at The Crown with George and Margaret for eight pm. It was gone 7.30 already. Emma stared at her reflection in the mirror, ran the comb through her hair one last time and threw Michael a scornful look.

"Yes," she snapped, scooping up her shoulder bag. She leant down and kissed Sam on the top of his head and marched in front of Michael out the front door. Michael shook his head in despair. He knew her mum's death and her father's loss were an added stress for Emma, but she was always so bloody wound up. It sometimes seemed to him that the only way she could relax was after several glasses of wine. He wondered if it was him that irritated her so much, but even when he made an effort to be patient and understanding, she still snapped. Mmm, patient and understanding, he now reflected guiltily. To be honest, he didn't make an effort. Not any more.

"Did you lock the back door, Mike?" asked Emma as she slipped into the passenger side of their BMW, deliberately now softening her voice. She knew she'd been offhand with him.

"Yes." Michael reversed out the drive, twisting his head to look behind him and Emma noticed his hair thinning on the back of his head. She was sorry she'd been abrupt with him, but she wished he would show more consideration for her. It wasn't easy right now. She would have preferred Michael to be more – what? Loving, maybe. Loving…oh dear. Maybe that was her fault.

Another unspoken issue.

"I'm sorry about your mother," said Margaret. George nodded his commiserations too, and passed the menu over to Michael. Emma smiled politely and sipped her Martini. Margaret looked stunning. Her long blonde hair fell over creamy smooth shoulders, and an ivory low cut silk blouse over a white see-through bra exposed a faint hint of brown nipples. Emma silently winced with envy. Moreover, Michael seemed to be tripping over himself with attentive approval, showering compliments over Margaret to an embarrassing degree.

George ordered roast venison for himself and Margaret and two bottles of house wine. He was an easy-going and contented man who thrived on too many business meals and an ever expanding waistline. "Emma," smiled George, "what's it to be?"

Emma chose smoked salmon and Michael garlic spiked pork.

"Garlic, eh? Your amorous advances might be rebuffed tonight Mike!" laughed George.

"Oh, there won't be a problem there, George. I know where I stand with that." Michael threw Emma a sideways glance and Emma felt herself stiffen. "And thinking of Emma, perhaps we ought to order another bottle of wine."

Emma and Michael hadn't made love for over four months, the longest they'd ever gone. Neither knew why it had become a problem and now it was easier to avoid it and not talk about it.

George and Margaret looked at each other, keen to lighten the mood. "Anyway, how are Simon and Chloe?"

They had all been friends for about ten years. Simon had befriended their son, Reuben, at secondary school bringing them together, sharing the school's social activities, being involved with PTA meetings and raising funds for various events. Both boys had long since moved on, but the adults had kept up regular social contact. If Emma and Michael had been happier in their own relationship, Emma might have enjoyed their company more, but as it was she felt threatened by Margaret's sexuality and jealous of Michael's evident attraction to her.

By the time the meals arrived, Emma was glowing from her second glass of wine. She was aware from Michael's disapproving frown that he had noticed her drinking too quickly but she chose to ignore him.

George had also noticed, perhaps more sympathetically. "More wine, Emma?" he offered, refilling it anyway. "I guess it's hard going for you at the moment – how's your father coping?"

"Oh thank you," said Emma raising the glass to her lips. "It's too early really to say." Emma didn't want to talk about her problems, much as she appreciated George's concern, and changed track to what she incorrectly considered safer ground. "So, have you two booked next year's holiday yet, then?"

Margaret dabbed the corners of her lips with a serviette but not before Emma caught a momentary shifting stare that flickered between the three of them.

"Well, what a coincidence that you should mention that, Emma!" Michael laughed with artificial pleasure and surprise. "Funnily enough, George and I were only just talking at the bar about us joining them skiing sometime next year."

Emma ran a finger round the rim of her wine glass rapidly, staring at the small pool of liquid swirling round. Ah, so that's what the look was all about. George, Margaret and Michael had been scheming on a foursome skiing holiday. No way. Emma wouldn't even go on an aeroplane, let alone risk skiing. Fool for asking about holidays! Now she was cornered, humiliated. Michael knew she would never fly. He knew she loathed travel.

"Thought perhaps Austria or Switzerland," said George, "but Michael seemed to think you might not be too keen?"

No. She might not be too keen, thank you Michael.

"Oh I can't plan for myself that far ahead…" Emma flushed uncomfortably. Yet she knew her fears were unfair, unreasonable.

"It would be such fun!" enthused Margaret, "You've never had a holiday without the children and never abroad, have you?"

True. Emma couldn't even be persuaded to catch a ferry to France. Fortunately, she'd met little resistance previously as Michael's job took him overseas, and he occasionally enjoyed golfing weekends with George in Europe. The children had travelled abroad with the school in the past and were now making independent plans anyway. But this was awful.

"Leave her," sighed Michael resignedly, "We'll talk later."

Margaret and George nodded politely. A waiter came and took their plates away.

"When's the funeral?" asked Margaret softly, keen to show consideration.

"Next Thursday."

A silence held them all briefly, then George piped up with news of an imminent business trip. "New York!" he boasted. "Never been, really looking forward to it. Hope to clinch a deal with Fosters – they're pretty keen on our product. Ever been, Mike?"

"No, I haven't. I envy you. You stayed there once, didn't you Emma?" asked Michael.

"Yes. Yes, I did."

"I didn't know that!" said Margaret, "when was this?"

"Oh late sixties. All hippy stuff!" Emma laughed "Stayed for about a month in Manhattan."

Both George and Margaret looked amazed. "Could there be a dark horse lurking in there somewhere? A secret past?" said George, leaning back as the waiter brought three Black Forest Gateaux to the table. Emma hadn't wanted one.

"Mmm," she said quietly, "maybe you'd be quite astounded."

The drive to Newcastle seemed endless. The rain lashed down in torrents and both Chloe and Simon fidgeted uncomfortably in the back. It was their first funeral, but they were happy to be together, and looking forward to seeing Uncle Steven.

Emma's brother Steven had been terribly distressed to hear of their mother's death and had said he'd try and get a standby ticket for a flight to England as soon as possible to attend the funeral. She thought it a shame he was prepared to make such an effort to come to the funeral – and yet not manage a visit in the last five years while she was alive, but she was looking forward to seeing him again.

Once the service was over, about a dozen relatives and friends, some unfamiliar to Emma, congregated at her dad's home for tea and biscuits. Steven looked well though much older. They were never close, but it was good to see him. It seemed a shame Mum wasn't there to see everyone.

"Okay Dad?" Emma put her arm round her father's waist and gave him a reassuring hug. He seemed overwhelmed, cocooned by family and friends yet isolated. The little terraced house had never been so full. It seemed an intrusion into his solitary space, welcome and unwelcome.

"Yes love. I'm fine," he sniffed, returning a wan smile. "Funny this, isn't it? Us all together. It's a good job your mother's not here," he whispered into her ear tossing a look discreetly behind him, "she'd loved to have seen young Steve again – but not all this crowd."

Emma smiled and briefly kissed him on the cheek. The action made her realize she hadn't kissed him on the cheek for years. Come to think of it, when had she last kissed Michael?

"Okay Pop?" Michael joined them, tea and two biscuits in hand. "Difficult time, isn't it?" He said softly.

Emma looked at Michael's cheek. She wondered about the feel of his skin under her lips. God, he was a stranger to her these days.

"Aye, it'll take a bit of getting used to."

"Where are Simon and Chloe, Michael? asked Emma.

"I think they've wandered into the kitchen to escape."

Emma squeezed her dad's hand. "Back in a tic. Just see what they're up to." She left her father talking with Michael and went into the small kitchen. Sure enough, Simon and Chloe were there with uncle Steven laughing at the photos on the mantelpiece.

"Bit out of date, isn't it Mum?" grinned Simon.

"I know. I must get a more recent photo."

This kitchen. This table. The chair. The sink. Mum had stood there once, pale and drawn, her hands dripping water onto the floor. "Oh my God," she had said. Now she was dead.

"You seem to be getting on better with Dad now," said Steven lightly. His life belonged thousands of miles away.

"Yes I guess so – and living in Cambridge means we can't see too much of each other and drive each other nuts!"

"And you've changed too."

"Have I?" Steven and Emma looked at each other. Chloe and Simon breezed off into the living room for a bite to eat.

"You seem quite staid in your middle age, serious. Probably easier for Dad to handle you these days."

"Are these insults, big brother?" Emma forced a smile, but was unsure how to take it. They held each other's gaze; so much unsaid. He held the power to destroy her marriage and throw her family into chaos. He knew it too.

Steven laughed, "No, not really. Michael okay? The business?"

"Fine!" smiled Emma dismissively, "and your 'better half'?"

24

"Fine." Steven grinned, nodding acknowledgement at each other's reticence. He paused a while, slowly casting his eyes around the small kitchen. "Brings things back a bit, all this, doesn't it?"

"Do you want me to take you and fetch you back?"

"No that's silly," said Emma stiffly. "There's fresh ham in the fridge, two vegetarian microwaveable curries in the cupboard and a well stocked freezer. Oh, and don't forget to feed Sam."

"Uh huh." The glasses perched precariously as he scribbled in another crossword clue.

Emma checked the contents of her weekend bag once more, but it was a delaying tactic before one last question. "That is – if you're staying in over the weekend?"

Michael looked up at Emma above the half moon of his glasses. "What do you mean?"

"Oh, I just wondered if you might nip over to George and Margaret's for a bite. And if you did, perhaps to check Chloe's got her keys." That didn't quite make sense. They both knew that, but the implication was understood. Their eyes met, they knew they should hug before she left but somehow even that kind of physical contact had become awkward. Emma wondered if Michael wanted to glimpse Margaret's nipples again or any other part of her anatomy.

"I've no idea what I'm doing. Haven't given it a thought, it's only a weekend."

"Yes. Okay, I'm off then." She picked up her bag and very lightly forced a cold kiss across his face. She hardly touched him.

"Drive carefully. Give me a ring when you get there." His eyes returned to the crossword. She closed the front door noisily as a gesture of annoyance and felt like crying. After she'd gone, Michael put the paper down and sighed heavily. What was wrong?

Jack hadn't touched Kathleen's side of the wardrobe since she'd died. Everything was just hanging there still. Emma suddenly wanted her mum to be there. Wanted a hug. She wished they had been closer. It was too late now. She glanced around her parents' bedroom; she could feel her mother's presence and wondered if she was there in spirit. That scared Emma less than the drive home.

She took the dresses from the coat hangers one by one, respectfully folding them neatly into the prepared suitcase. She placed her nose into the fabric of a once familiar dress.

After about an hour, Emma started on the handbags in the bottom of the wardrobe. It seemed her mum had kept every bag she'd ever owned. Emma opened each one to ensure they were clean and empty before putting them in the charity shop pile. The odd one had a freshly laundered handkerchief, a redundant purse or an old shopping list. The process seemed an intrusion of privacy and such a rude act of dismissal.

At first, Emma thought nothing of the bag containing an old diary, even though it was more carefully preserved, wrapped in brown paper. She flipped idly through the blank pages. 1981. Obviously some unwanted gift tucked absently away. Right at the end, Emma noticed a faded piece of newspaper meticulously folded in half. She opened it. It was an old cutting saved from a personal announcement in a daily paper. Emma looked at it with mild curiosity…

> *BIRTHS BY ADOPTION: Brandon, Colin and Mary are pleased to announce the arrival of their son, Julian Marc, by adoption.*

Emma sat on the edge of the bed staring at it. The word adoption pounced out at her but the names meant nothing. Who could they be? Why had her mum kept this announcement? 1981? What happened then? Emma tried to pin some importance to the year, but nothing clicked. Colin and Mary Brandon meant nothing to her. Then again, the newspaper clipping didn't necessarily belong to 1981. Her eyes moved to the top of the yellowed page.

February 1967

Birth by adoption? Oliver was born in November 1966. It took three months for the official papers to be signed. No…surely? She felt furtive, secretive – she shouldn't know this. How did Mum know? Did Emma have a son somewhere, called Julian Marc Brandon, twenty-eight years old? The name felt strange to her.

She became aware that her father was calling her. She folded up the newspaper cutting, placed it back in the diary for safe keeping, and put the diary in her pocket. She patted the small bulge to make sure it was there, her emotions checked for the time being, and called down to her father. "Thanks Dad, just coming..."

Part Two

1966

Chapter Two

Emma stirred her cornflakes round and round the bowl. They tasted like bits of cardboard. A bit of milk splattered onto the yellow formica table and Emma circled it with her finger as if to rub it in.

Although her movements were slow and deliberate, her heart raced as she watched Mum washing pots at the kitchen sink. The gentle slapping of water, the clatter of plates on the draining board, the soft hum of song from her lips.

A few last seconds of calm before the blast.

"Mum..." Emma's voice sounded disembodied, distant. This was awful. Her throat felt so dry she had to push the words out. "I think I'm pregnant."

I think I'm pregnant.

The thinly whispered confession screamed through the small kitchen paralysing them with silence, save for the rhythmic, slow tick of the kitchen clock on the tiled mantelpiece.

Kathleen swung round, one hand clutching the sink for support, the other dangling, wet, dripping onto the floor. The impact was immediate – Emma saw the ashen face stare back at her. No more slapping of water. No more humming. For a moment the stillness held them in rigid suspense.

"Oh my God. How late are you?"

"Two days."

Emma looked down from her mother's frightened glare and watched a drop of water fall onto the floor from her hand. She heard her sigh briefly as if "two days" offered some respite or allowed a safe margin of error.

"Thank goodness," said Emma's mother, now wiping both hands dry on the apron as if trying to establish order and make everything all right. "You can't possibly know... I mean, have you...?"

31

Emma glanced back up again. She felt sick. The walls seemed to sway, everything was wobbly, and panic reeled within her at the shock of her own voice as much as the reality of what she had said.

"Have you – have you slept with him?"

"Sort of."

"What do you mean – 'sort of'?" It was offered as a plea to remove the threat, correct the mistake, render the confession absurd.

"Well, nearly…"

Emma and her mother stared at each other hopelessly. "Oh you silly bairn! For God's sake, just take this as a warning. Go to school and everything will be all right by the time you come home. But goodness, you be careful in future."

Dismissed.

Emma stood up and pushed the bowl of cornflakes away. A strange embarrassment locked them both in their separate thoughts. Perhaps stupidly, the revelation that Emma had had sex seemed to override the possible consequences and now silence offered privacy once more. Emma's mother turned again to the sink, immersing her hands in the soapy water. Go to school and everything will be all right by the time you come home. But it wasn't going to be all right.

Emma was seventeen, studying for her A levels – and pregnant.

Later that day, Emma huddled in the arms of her boyfriend in a telephone kiosk down a quiet, poor backstreet in Newcastle-upon-Tyne. Insulated from the cold, biting wind outside, they held each other; John opened his donkey jacket to envelope Emma more closely. They spoke in whispers, although there was no-one to hear them. John and Emma often spent private moments in telephone kiosks, cocooned in their own intimate space. Outside, the street was littered with rubbish, the wall covered with obscene graffiti and a fallen dustbin spewed fish and chips remains.

"Are you sure?" He breathed the words so quietly they were almost inaudible.

"I'm never late, John. Never."

"But you can't be, we've not really done it properly."

Emma said nothing. Both she and John stood quietly holding one another.

"We can't get married," John whispered. "I mean, I want us to stay together but we're too young to get married." He sounded frightened. She could hear his heart racing as he cradled her head into his chest. Emma slid her arms around his body, under his chunky black jumper. His soft voice reverberated into her cushioned face, his breath warm. She noticed the small windows furring with condensation.

"I know, I know. It's okay. I'm not asking you to marry me." Neither of them knew what they wanted. They held each other, his hand nervously stroking her hair, both scared and insecure. She could smell his skin, feel his square chin resting on her head, and nestled more tightly into his chest.

"We'll be okay," he offered weakly, as much to reassure himself as Emma. "It'll be okay…"

"Of course, you'll have to leave school."

Her mother had taken on an authoritative role. Still no period and yesterday's news had penetrated her protective wall of denial. Emma sat in the same chair in the kitchen as yesterday morning. The kitchen had always been a hub of family communication: even when Steven had lived at home, it had always been where they'd congregate to share news, talk through problems, discuss plans. 37 Boulter Street was an end terrace on the corner of Jarrow Street. A small, pre-war three up and three down, each room small and dark, yet secure. Emma had lived there since birth, her very being rooted into its foundations, the kitchen the safest haven on earth, until now.

"That is, if you're right and you're pregnant. And what about John? What does he say about all this?" Mum stood facing her, leaning against the sink; one blue plastic roller under her hair net.

Emma looked down into her lap, tears stinging the back of her eyes, the naughty girl being told off. She mumbled acknowledgement that she would have to leave school and softly tried to protect John, who both her parents loathed anyway, reassurring her mother that he would stand by her.

"Stand by you?! Oh hinny! I should say so too!" Her mother sank heavily into a chair next to her and held Emma's small, shaking hands. "You silly bairn, you silly, silly bairn. Didn't you know... didn't you think?" she sighed helplessly, too uncomfortable to interrogate her daughter about specific sexual intimacies, "Oh well, I guess we're going to have to work this one out and see what we can do. If you are...if you are pregnant, will John marry you?"

"I don't think we want to get married." In truth, Emma would have liked to marry John; even the thought of having his baby already seemed to fill a primary sense of longing, but she understood he felt too young to be tied down. That they were both too young, too immature.

"It might be a case of him having to do the decent thing, you know." Emma's mother raised her eyebrows, her voice edged with discipline in an attempt to conceal fear. "We don't have many choices. Have you given any thought to the future?"

Emma hadn't. Well, not really. It was silly, because she was excited at being pregnant. Like having a puppy for Christmas. Yet she knew, too, it wasn't quite like that.

"Perhaps you've heard of someone who's been in a similar mess, and er, tried to solve things? Obviously, one has to be careful. But there are ways... Then of course, there's adoption."

What was going on? To Emma, the situation seemed unreal. The problem of having created a new life seemed out of her grasp. It was confusing because the dilemma held underlying joy, but also, she felt unable to see its long-term repercussions.

"And God knows what your father will say." Emma's mother shook her head despairingly. The vision of her sweet young daughter overwhelmed with irresistible sexual urges, fumbling with passion, filled her with disgust, disapproval and envy all at once.

The thought of her father's reaction filled Emma with dread. He was not a loving man, always disgruntled and tired, moaning over the newspaper every evening about some injustice or another. He worked long hours on low pay, insisting on a weekly breakdown of expenditure from his wife before giving her housekeeping money on a Friday night. He was as economical with his affections as his money. God knows what her father would say.

Emma had met John in a quayside coffee bar six months previously in August 1965. She had been with her best friend, Katy, on one of their regular "about town" haunts with the specific intent of meeting boys. It was the era of Mary Quant and Twiggy. Emma thought Katy looked rather like Mary Quant with a sharp, geometrically chopped bob round an urchin face, while she herself emulated Twiggy. In fact, Emma looked more as if she had tumbled out of a sunshine cereal packet: her straight, chin length rich amber hair delicately framed a tawny complexion and large limpid brown eyes peered innocently above a button nose. The only likeness to Twiggy was her waif-like appearance. But John had immediately been drawn to her slender femininity and, along with his friend, Jeffrey, had soon introduced himself. The Beatles droned from the jukebox as they shared espressos and small talk. John, too, was studying for his A levels at a city grammar school and planning on applying to university. In contrast to Emma, he was big boned, blond yet strong featured with striking blue eyes. Emma felt he was like a Nordic god; his soft, penetrating stare later revealed an aloof intelligence. She told him her hopes of attending Newcastle College to study fashion design and he shared his dreams with her. They were completely absorbed with each other, totally ignoring Katy and Jeffrey.

If there is such a thing as love at first sight, this was it. By the end of the evening, they left the coffee bar holding hands.

Two weeks went by and at home little more had been said. It seemed Emma's mum was waiting for 'the right time' to tell her father. As Emma lay in the bath one night, she gently caressed her stomach, marveling with disbelief at the small life that lay within her. The first pangs of maternal bonding swept through her and she smiled to herself, instinctively feeling him to be a boy.

"Don't worry, my babe," she said softly, patting her still flat tummy. "I'll look after you. We'll be all right, you and me."

A temporary calm both at home and with John allowed space for Emma to pretend her baby was a treasured secret. And no-one else knew, except Katy. A virgin, Katy had been as thrilled as her, delighted with her best friend's ultimate consummation of love, hounding her with questions of intercourse as much as pregnancy. "What's it like?" she had begged, admitting to still struggling with tampons.

Emma stretched her foot to the end of the bath and turned on the hot tap with her big toe. Slowly she washed her swollen breasts, seeing the newly darkened nipples. A stranger to her own body, she revered herself as a sacred tomb, a sensual woman. Now with no further need to be "careful", she and John had succumbed to their hungry demands and made love time and time again. She loved John even more deeply, more needfully, and it seemed wonderful to be pregnant.

John, too, was proud – but guarded. On the one hand, he felt a man – mature, a father-to-be; yet on the other, he was desperate for freedom. Emma and John didn't speak of the future. For the moment, everything was on pause. They knew, soon, they would be at the mercy of Emma's family.

Emma got out of the bath, dried herself and put on her pink pyjamas and dressing gown then went downstairs to make a hot milk before going to bed. As soon as she opened the living room door, the atmosphere chilled her to the bone. Emma met her father's gaze, staring coldly over the rim of his glasses without raising his head from the newspaper.

"Your mother's told me."

"Oh…"

"You stupid girl."

"I'm sorry…" Emma dropped her head and shuffled her feet.

"Is he going to do the decent thing and marry you?"

"Er, no…he – we don't want to get married."

"What do you propose to do, then?"

"I don't know, Dad." Emma looked like a twelve-year-old in her night clothes, and under her father's harsh glare, she felt it.

"You've given your mother a lot of heartache. We didn't need this, Emma. What have John's parents said?" He folded his newspaper and glared at her.

"He doesn't want them to know. He said they'd go berserk and take over, that it would be a nightmare for everyone, that they'd interfere, keep the baby and stop John going to university and…"

Recoiling at this scenario, Emma's father interrupted her, feigning understanding. "Well, what do you want?"

"I don't know." Emma started to cry.

"You can't keep it. That's out of the question. There's no way your mother can start rearing another wee bairn after all these years while you go idling the rest of your misspent youth away. A right mess you've put us all in, haven't you?"

Emma's mother quietly joined them, no doubt having timed her appearance deliberately. Emma rushed into her arms and sobbed, her mum responded protectively. "Ssh, shh, there there now, hinny." Swaying slightly in a soft, rocking motion, Emma's mother patted her daughter in a close embrace. "But we do need to work out what we should do and I think perhaps we should get in touch with a social worker soon."

"I've told her she can't keep it." Emma's father had suddenly feared for his own future. At forty-seven, with one daughter of seventeen and a married son, Steven, twenty-three, he envisaged years ahead without so much hardship. Life had not been easy for them, money had been tight and they'd gone without too many times because of the children. Now, at long last, he dreamed of holidays, abroad even – perhaps Spain or France – and buying a more modern car. A twelve month hiccup would be bad enough – but there was no way he could accept another addition to the family.

During the next few weeks, Emma dismissed her mother's hint of gin and hot baths, accepted John's need for lack of involvement, succumbed to her father's total rejection of anything to do with "it" and, as soon as the pregnancy was medically confirmed, was visited by a social worker from the Adoption Society.

Miss Smith looked the part: a straight laced spinster. Endeavouring not to pass judgement, she forced a patronising smile. It was hard to tell whether she was thirty or sixty, the stiff, tweed skirt decently covering most of her heavy legs but revealing sensible brogue lace up shoes. A plain hair grip scraped her brown hair to the side enabling her to study the official form on her lap.

"We need some details first," she said in impeccable BBC English. "Now, it's Emma Hargreaves, isn't it?"

Emma's mother warmed to the social worker immediately, impressed with the educated accent and classic country attire. She became more upright and spoke more correctly in an effort to join ranks. Emma felt embarrassed and out of place. She knew that the Powers that Be had to take over and that she was duty bound to be subservient; she didn't want more recriminations and disapproval. She answered their questions obediently.

The plan of action was that Miss Smith would try to find a maternity hospital prepared to accept Emma as an unmarried mother, and then Emma would relinquish her baby for fostering at ten days old, followed by subsequent adoption at six weeks. After another six weeks, almost three and a half months after the baby's birth, Emma would need to sign papers affirming that she had legally and completely given up the child, that in effect, her baby now belonged to new parents. Miss Smith went on to explain the careful selection procedure employed in finding suitable parents. She told Emma about the many couples wanting to provide a secure, loving home for a baby who were sadly unable to have their own children. She explained that it would be in the best interests of the child, that Emma could feel completely safe knowing she had done the "correct thing" – and relieved herself and her parents from untold social condemnation, disgrace and financial hardship.

Emma listened. It seemed such an obvious solution, yet she felt uneasy. She was reassured that her smeared reputation could be rebuilt, that she would be able to go forward, even marry and have children of her own one day and that this present "accident" would all be behind her. Forgotten. She nodded in the right places and obligingly allowed herself to be drawn into the scheme of things.

But that night in bed, Emma cradled her stomach, now just slightly bigger, and cried into the pillow. She slept fitfully; everything seemed out of her control.

George Green & Co was a shoe factory two bus journeys away from her house. She had lied at the interview, saying that financial circumstance meant she could no longer continue at school and that she needed to contribute to family income. The personnel manager had listened sympathetically, approving of Emma's obvious sense of duty and offered her the vacant position in a small office. General office work, filing and routine administrative procedures as required. Emma walked away, pleased she had got the job, yet humiliated and bored already at the prospect of the menial tasks involved.

"I'm scared, John." Emma snuggled into her boyfriend and stared blankly through the steamed up windows of the telephone kiosk.

"You'll be okay," he offered reassuringly. "You didn't like school anyway. Said you were fed up with studying."

"Aye, I know, but I feel so kind of useless now. Like I'm a failure. I had all those dreams of being a fashion designer, and now what? Nearly eighteen, pregnant, working in some pathetic office in a shoe factory. And what about – what will it be like?"

"You mean the birth?" John felt uncomfortable. He didn't want to talk about that. He didn't want to talk about the pregnancy at all.

"Na, silly billy," Emma giggled slightly. "I mean this new job, and then telling them, and I don't know, just losing everything."

John held her tightly and kissed her silky hair. Burying his nose into its warm, baby softness always made him want her. "You won't lose me," he murmured. His thoughts had turned towards other matters; Emma sensed this and tilted her face towards him. A hollow sensation in her stomach mingled with fear and desire.

"You know what I'd really love?"

"What?" John was now highly attentive.

"A pickled gherkin."

Shit. This was a mess. Emma tried to visualize a year ahead. She was now two months pregnant. It was April, the baby was due mid-November. In twelve months it would be over; the pregnancy, the birth, the adoption...what had Miss Smith said? That this present 'accident' would be all behind her. Forgotten.

Chapter Three

Just as Emma's own life seemed to be shrinking, John's was expanding. He had already attended three interviews for university and there were more to come. A levels were imminent and for the summer he and a few of his friends were planning a couple of months travelling around Europe. "I'll come back bronzed and irresistible!" he had teased. "You won't be able to keep your hands off me." Their respective futures were diverging and their relationship was becoming increasingly lop-sided.

Moreover, as news of Emma's pregnancy spread, many friends sheepishly kept their distance, encouraged by disapproving parents. Katy stood by her as her closest ally, but otherwise it became a lonely existence.

It was Katy who had given Emma the address of a so-called herbalist allegedly willing to 'help' young pregnant girls and although Emma knew she would never abort her baby, she liked the thought of owning some control of the situation. Just the thought of not necessarily having to do what she was told seemed like an escape route. She was feeling trapped and tears came easily and frequently, driving John further into his need for freedom. He reassured Emma time and time again that he loved her, that he would stay around, that she wasn't losing him – but Emma was on a downer.

And work at George Greens & Co. was infinitely more boring than she could possibly have imagined; tying elastic bands around bundles of fifty filing cards then filing the filing cards in a filing system in a filing cabinet. She shared the office with Sylvia and Elizabeth, two close-knit giggling girls in their twenties with emerald eyeshadow and white stiletto shoes. The factory was an old decrepit building stinking of leather and resin and although the office was situated on the top floor, both the smell and the noise of machinery droning constantly below infiltrated every corner.

Sylvia and Elizabeth sat in the middle of the office with their own typewriters, locked in conversation and only acknowledging Emma from time to time. The long hours were alleviated periodically by the office wolf, an acne riddled, bespectacled senior clerk who considered himself a Hank Marvin look-alike, swaggering in and out the office whistling *Strangers in the Night*. Emma was his latest target as he plied her with dubious compliments such as "And how's my little carrot today?"

However, the little carrot was growing. Golden and beautiful, maybe; but an expanding midriff would soon necessitate action – or a more honest confrontation with the personnel manager.

Emma walked up and down Lemington Gate pretending to idly gaze into the shop windows. It was an old, narrow Dickensian street with a row of three dingy shops sandwiched between terraced accommodation and derelict houses. The herbalist's front window consisted of several small grubby panes of glass. Peering through, she noticed shelves of brown bottles and the back of a man wearing a white smock busily rearranging them. Emma's eyes looked up and read the words:

ERIC BROWNE. APOTHECARY & HERBALIST

She shuddered. This was just role play, she knew. A morbid sense of drama eventually lured her through the heavy door. Opening the door made a bell ring and the white smock – a dirty white smock Emma now noticed – turned round to face her. "Can I help you?" queried the old man, stooped and resting a hand on the counter.

Emma had been told what to say.

"Er, I'm going on holiday soon and my period is due then. I wonder if you have anything to bring it on early?" Her voice sounded strange, like when she first told her mum she was pregnant.

"Mmm. I see. How late?" He peered at her intently, furrowing his brows. She noticed yellow nicotine stains on his grey moustache.

"About ten weeks."

"Mmm. I see." He wiped a grubby finger under his nose, frowning, then turned around, took a dark glass bottle from the top shelf and slowly counted out six large oatmeal coloured pills. "Take these, all in one go, first thing in the morning on an empty stomach." He methodically placed each round tablet into a paper bag, twisted the top and, as he passed them to Emma, leaned over the counter and breathed into her face. Emma could smell stale tobacco. "I should have the day off school if I was you."

Emma paid the man ten shillings and six pence, wincing at his easy recognition of her age, and left. Once outside, she could feel her heart thumping and a wave of nausea rose in her gullet.

As soon as she got home, she went into her bedroom. The house was empty but still she closed the door, wedging a pillow on the floor just in case her mother tried to come in. She opened the paper bag, picked out one of the large tablets – almost the size of a halfpenny – sniffed it and cautiously let the end of her tongue lightly brush the surface. An unpleasant chemical aftertaste lingered, making her shudder. She wondered how on earth anyone could swallow anything so large, but it didn't matter to her. Slowly, Emma placed the dampened pill back into the bag, went into the bathroom and dropped them one by one down the toilet before pulling the chain.

What a waste of money, she thought.

"Why didn't you say so in the first place?" The personnel manager peered at Emma, full of concern.

"I'm sorry. I needed the job and thought you wouldn't give it to me if I told you the truth." Still she kept her eyes away from him.

"What are you going to do, my dear?" He leaned back in his oak chair and spoke softly, without condemnation.

"The baby's going to be adopted. Then I don't know."

"That's what you want, is it?"

Emma felt the hollow sensation in her stomach again, and a pins and needles feeling tickled her nipples. The question confused and agitated her. It didn't have anything to do with what she wanted, did it? She said nothing.

"Well listen. I'm sorry about your…er, predicament, but I will help you in any way I can." The personnel manager looked troubled. "I understand you will need to leave us – let me think, September? But if you want to come back, er…afterwards, there will be a job here for you if you want."

Overwhelmed by his kindness, Emma stood up to leave. Her stomach rose slightly with the movement and a brief wave of self pity merged with indigestion. Words of concern and support were hard to come by. She thanked him very much and he rose from his seat to extend his hand. "Remember, anything I can do to help..."

It was not so easy finding a maternity hospital to accept her. Emma was unaware of the effort and humiliation encountered by the social worker, Miss Smith, and her mother as they made enquiries over a hospital stay for Emma's delivery. Miss Smith had strongly pointed out the advantages to both Emma and Mrs Hargreaves of the special homes available to unmarried mothers, but neither Emma nor her mother wanted this.

"It really is advisable to consider what is best for everyone all round," she had emphasized in her tut-tutting manner, stern eyebrow raised in reprimand. "You must think about yourself, Mrs Hargreaves, and your husband, a decent hard working man. If Emma were to be, shall we say 'removed' from home for a few months, on the pretext of visiting some aunt for example, then your neighbours need never know about this at all, which would be much easier for yourselves and for Emma. She could come home after the baby's been handed over, and get on with her life again, with no-one being any the wiser."

But Kathleen was worried about the strict discipline employed by such establishments and, although exhausted with despair and worry, she didn't want to disown her daughter. Moreover, this was going to be her first grandchild... A small knot twisted itself within her.

With the help of the family doctor and district nurse, an appointment was eventually made for Emma to visit the matron of Sykefield House Maternity Home.

Miss Bates was a colossal woman who reminded Emma of a settee: somehow, everything seemed more horizontal than vertical. Her stiffly starched uniform matched the grim face as she ordered Emma to take a seat, while she waddled round to face Emma on the other side of a huge table. The uniform crackled as she squeezed her fat bottom into the broad chair.

"So, you have disgraced your family, haven't you?" she said fiercely. "And why are you not getting married?"

Emma had not expected this. She thought there may be a few administrative formalities, a grumbling disapproval – but not immediate harsh condemnation. "Er, he…we don't want to," she whispered.

"My dear, it is hardly a case of 'we don't want to', is it? You are expecting a baby and in the eyes of God, you have sinned. The only decent thing you can do now is get married and have this child respectably. It is unlawful and evil to bring an illegitimate baby into this world. You have been a wicked, wicked foolish child and if your boyfriend loves you and respects you he will want to marry you."

Emma couldn't speak for tears choking her. She wanted to argue, protest, put forward another opinion and shout, "You're wrong! You're wrong!" – but she sat there, snivelling and ineffectual.

"I will have to consider whether it is right and proper for us to have you deliver a baby out of wedlock here. As a Christian, it is my duty to point out the gravity of your sins and that is why I was prepared to meet you. Unless you can comply with honouring your own responsibilities, I'm not sure we can be of help." Miss Bates paused for breath. "And what, pray, had you in mind for your baby?"

"It's going to be adopted." Emma spoke in staccato gulps, her cheeks wet from tears.

The room smelled unpleasantly of the matron's stale perspiration and dark rings circled the fabric under her armpits. Her huge bosom swelled as she took an even bigger intake of breath, hoisting them higher by assertively folding her fat arms underneath. Shaking her head, she issued instructions, "No, no no, my dear. You have created a life between you and you must get married. However," she continued, effectively dismissing Emma's words as worthless, "in the eyes of the Lord I may consider some leniency in this disgraceful situation if you make a further appointment to see me with your boyfriend."

Emma recoiled, tears streaming down her face. This was a nightmare. Of course John wouldn't come; and if he did, he wouldn't sit there like she did, all weeping and drippy. He would probably call Miss Bates a self righteous, pompous, fat old bag. But he wouldn't come anyway. That was stupid. It was all stupid and awful. Emma sat there and sobbed, so much so that snatched intakes of breath made catching, choking sounds.

The matron wheezed herself out the chair and panted towards the door. "I will get a nurse to take you somewhere private until you've composed yourself, then you must go home. I will wait for you to be in touch." With that, she creaked and groaned her settee form out of the door.

"Oh Mum," wailed Emma, "I can't possibly have my baby there! The matron was awful... Oh please don't make me – I'd rather die!"

Kathleen stood the iron on its end, reached over to switch the plug off and sighed deeply. She felt tired, so tired. At times she was angry with Emma for having created this problem, yet she knew that her daughter may have been quite ignorant in matters of birth control. They had never really discussed it, and John was not the kind of young man that encouraged Emma's mother to want to talk – well, about that sort of thing.

"Oh dear. I really don't know what to say."

"Please let me stay here, please say I can have the baby at home."

"At home? Oh my love, I don't know about that – what on earth would your father say?"

"Please Mum, please..." Emma was distraught. Her pleading, large brown eyes were filled with urgency. The only way to console her was to promise to look into it. Secretly, Kathleen was worried about other things; how Jack would react. She was having problems with him anyway. Then there was the fear that she herself would end up nursing the new born baby until it was fostered. How would she feel when it left? Yet no-one thought about her. She was doing a delicate juggling act trying to hold everything together: keeping Jack happy, consoling Emma, thinking of what was best for the baby... It seemed her own feelings didn't matter. She was just useful in making everyone else's life bearable.

Kathleen wrapped the flex around the iron, folded the ironing board and put them both away in the pantry. All the time she could feel her daughter's eyes following her. "Please Mum..."

"We'll have a word with the doctor, Emma. See what the situation is and then I'll talk to your father."

John and Emma lay naked on the bed, John exhaling on his cigarette and both of them watching the spirals of smoke drift towards the ceiling. They hadn't got under the covers to make love as that seemed an intrusion of Paul's privacy. Paul was a friend who had a bedsit and 'loaned' his room out to close friends occasionally, in exchange for cash or favours – whichever was the greater need. Bob Dylan wailed morosely from the wireless *The Times They Are A-Changing.*

"All being well, I'll get into Leeds, then I can come back at weekends to see you." John drew hard on the remaining stub. "I just don't want to fuck up my A levels. It's the stupid piece on Virginia Woolf that worries me."

Emma turned on her side towards him, sliding her hand up and down his lean body. She loved the way his chest dipped down to his stomach, firm with a slight dusting of blond hair. "You'll be fine," she said softly, feeling loved enough for the moment. The warm smell of his body, of sex, of cigarettes, enveloped her in a sensuous calm.

"Yeah, let's hope so." He put out his cigarette and rolled towards her, running his fingers down her small nose playfully. Emma screwed up her face. "I shall miss you when I go to Europe. Don't go getting into mischief now, will you?"

"Hardly, in my condition!" This Europe thing niggled her a bit. She wished he would spend the summer with her.

"Ah, but in your condition you can get away with it."

"What about you and your friends bumming it around Amsterdam and Sweden?"

"I won't even look at another girl." John tussled her hair and grinned mischievously. Emma went quiet. If only feeling loved enough lasted a bit longer. Maybe she was just jealous that his life was free and full of adventure, and hers was so confined. Yet she liked being pregnant. She felt well and loved the tiny bundle within her. But, ultimately, she was sad, trapped and, yes, jealous. Not just of John, but of Katy too, having just been accepted at Newcastle College to study fashion design, the very course Emma had wanted to take. The syllabus promised haute and wholesale couture, design research, pattern making, illustration and travel – Carnaby Street and Barbara Hulanicki's BIBA Boutique in London with a Paris trip on the horizon.

And vulnerable. Bruised already from "society's" rejection, humiliated by her exit from school and embarrassed with her pregnancy, Emma wanted more reassurance and affection from John, who was too preoccupied with his own evolving future to give it.

"Anyway, while I'm away it gives you the perfect chance to read Kafka and Sartre; if you have time try Salinger and Kerouac – plus the works of Oscar Wilde."

"Excuse me, but I'm not being left behind to undertake some literary exercise!"

"Do you good, ideal opportunity to broaden your mind." He kissed her nose. "You don't read enough."

It was true. Sometimes she struggled to keep up with what he laughingly called "his superior intellect". Really, she would have preferred more cuddles, more reassurance, more words of affection...but he always rationalized everything. Even love. She always wanted more. He called her over-emotional and insecure.

He reached over to the cigarette packet and took out another cigarette. After lighting it, he offered it to Emma. She shook her head and John once again lay flat on his back, gazing at the ceiling, wrapped in his own thoughts. Emma lay her arm over his chest, silent too, feeling his heartbeat, watching the smoke float to the ceiling, listening to the wireless and unsure as to whether she was happy or sad.

Suddenly, something happened inside her.

Emma froze. It stopped.

Then it happened again. Like a butterfly in her stomach, quite defined.

Emma remained motionless, every nerve in her body now focused on this new sensation. At first she said nothing and John lay there, inhaling deeply, unaware of Emma's suspense.

It happened once more and Emma shattered their silence. "What on earth's that?" she burst out.

"What's what?" John froze now, too, catching her tension.

"Inside – something happened. Really strange – like a big nervous kind of tickle, all wriggly, just here..." Emma took John's hand and placed it gently, palm down, on her stomach. "I know what it was! Oh John! It was the baby! I just felt him move – I just felt my baby move!!"

Emma got her way. It was arranged she would have a home delivery and she was assigned her own midwife. Emma liked Mrs Lacey immediately; she was younger than her own mother, maybe in her mid-thirties, slim, pretty, with a fresh, open and honest look about her. A slight fragrance of soap made everything about her seem home grown, clean and natural.

It was only a brief first meeting. They would be much more involved with each other towards the end of Emma's pregnancy. But that was fine. Emma was well, the baby seemed to be thriving and Emma's mother was just relieved to have Emma a little more settled. However, it was going to be a chore sterilizing all the necessary equipment. The midwife would give her a list of everything required at a later date – and then, of course, there would have to be all the preparations for confinement. They had no central heating so some form of heating, at least in the bedroom, would be important; the floor, fortunately, was already linoleum though maybe a rag rug would lend some degree of comfort, also jugs and bowls were plentiful, there was a plain sideboard which could be useful and a couple of spare chairs – oh, and somewhere wasn't there still a rubber undersheet that could go on the bed?

The practicalities of childbirth were of no consequence to Emma. The most immediate problem to her was that she had nothing left to wear. It was the end of July, she was nearly six months pregnant. Her hair was now shoulder length and she ironed it to make it straighter. She wore pale lipstick and glued bits of false eyelash to both top and bottom lashes in addition to the fine black lines painted just beneath her eyes – but she could not get into her normal clothes. Her mum had sewn up a couple of loose shift dresses in cheap crimplene from the market instead. Emma drooled over the radical, new fashion trends and fantasized over her image once the birth was behind her. Completely familiar now with her baby's constant movements, it was as if she had always been pregnant and always would be. Perhaps it was immaturity – or avoidance – but the reality of labour, of bearing her own flesh and blood, a real little human being, seemed to escape her. Emma's mum didn't talk to her about the baby. The practicalities were discussed, but not the adoption, not feelings. Best not to. For everyone's sake.

John had gone on his European travels and was due to return within the month. He had kept up a regular correspondence – but, of course, as soon as he came back he would be preparing to start his sociology and economics course at Leeds. Emma's parents, especially her mother, welcomed his absence. They found John arrogant and unapproachable. Emma seemed easily manipulated by his patronizing attitude.

Kathleen had once insinuated her disapproval and Emma had erupted into tears, screaming and accusing her of parental ignorance. It had created further distance between her and her daughter. No, it was best to keep quiet. Emma's father felt the same. In fact they took it one step further and didn't discuss their daughter between themselves, either. Just for good measure.

Emma had only four weeks left at George Green & Co., then it would be a case of antenatal classes and biding her time until November. Emma didn't know whether Sylvia and Elizabeth had officially been told about her pregnancy, or whether they'd deduced the fact from her appearance. Either way little changed except their giggles became more furtive, their occasional acknowledgement of Emma more sympathetic and, she was sure, their eyeshadow even more emerald green. The predicted date for her baby's arrival was November 13th. Everything had been arranged: the home birth, the midwife, the preliminary fostering and then adoption… It had all been taken care of. All Emma had to do was plod on until it was over.

"Oh Emma, come on – it will be a real giggle! Seriously, it would do you good to get out. And it's Otis Redding live; afterwards you can stop over at my place. Mum won't mind, she still really likes you." Katy was persuading Emma to go to a gig on Saturday at the Casino Dance Hall. It had been ages since she'd been to a dance – and she had always loved to burn away the hours gyrating almost trance-like in a world of her own.

"But what on earth can I wear? Look at me!" Emma stood up, chuckling, and pushed her stomach out in exaggerated fashion. Katy lay sprawled on Emma's bed, her long, skinny legs dangling over the edge. She was pretty, with smiling eyes beaming from under a heavy, dark fringe. She tossed back her thick bobbed hair and laughed. "Let's have a look…"

Between them, they spent several hours sorting through Emma's wardrobe. Emma stripped and changed clothes again and again, armed with scissors for necessary dress surgery while they both giggled and played like young children dressing up. Emma hadn't had such fun for months. It was almost a relief at times, not having John around. She could act silly and not be frowned upon, make high pitched squeals and pull funny faces, drop any image of decorum and intelligence – and just be Emma. She had almost forgotten her playful side. Emma's mother downstairs could hear the two girls and smiled to herself.

The dance hall was packed and in the dim lights Emma's pregnancy was concealed and she and Katy were inundated with suitors. The two girls kept sneaking furtive glances at one another and falling into helpless laughter as young men made optimistic advances. They finally left at two am, catching a taxi back to Katy's.

"Oh Emma, what a scream!" cried Katy as she struggled to put coffee into mugs. "That one with the beard – he was all over you!"

"I know, and my baby was kicking like crazy, he must have thought my stomach was riddled with worms or something!" The pair of them collapsed into chairs at the kitchen table, remembering now to be quiet so as not to wake Katy's mum.

"Was it? How weird. So your baby's been to his first disco." Katy paused and cradled her coffee. "Emma, what will you do?"

"What do you mean, 'what will I do?' " She caught Katy's sober tone.

"I don't know what I mean. But it's a big thing, isn't it? I mean, joking apart, it's a bloody big upheaval."

Emma suddenly felt weepy. Maybe it was the cider, or exhaustion, (she was sure she shouldn't really have danced like that or drank so much at six months) or hormones. Maybe it was justified. She wasn't used to being confronted and it caught her off guard.

"I don't know, Katy." Emma shrugged her shoulders. "I've even thought about ending it with John when the baby's adopted and maybe going to live in London."

"That sounds a bit like running away."

"No," said Emma. "It's making a fresh start."

"You can't finish with John. You two are made for each other – you know you love him."

"But so much has been unfair this last year. And now after his holiday, he's off to university. Where am I in all this? Silly fat pregnant doormat, always waiting for his return. I need some life of my own, and I can't have it with John – it feels sometimes like I'm just a convenience, an accessory. And I can't help but feel resentful and jealous, which is no good for either of us."

"But what about John? He would be devastated at losing you."

"Would he? I wonder."

"Emma! Of course he would. I know it's difficult at the moment, but just think ahead. Soon you'll be slim and free again, able to go wherever you want…to Leeds so you can be together if you like, or you could apply for the fashion design course again or even just get a good job. You could go back to George Greens & Co. for a while."

Emma stuck her fingers down her throat and faked a vulgar throwing up sound. Katy laughed. "But you know what I mean," she said, "I know it feels bloody awful at the moment, but things will get better."

"Oh Katy, I don't know. I can't go to college now; I've flunked my A levels. All I've got is four miserable O levels and a bad reputation. And please don't lumber me with a future at George Greens & Co. I'd rather die!"

"Maybe you'll see things differently when the baby's…" she tried to choose her words carefully but changed her line of thought instead. "What about the baby? How do you feel about it?"

Emma felt a tug. It shocked her. There was a sharp pain. "I don't know. I just don't know."

Walking away from George Green & Co. was quite sad. The personnel manager had called her into his office to wish her all the best and reiterate his offer of work should she ever need it; even the office wolf gave her an affectionate squeeze and said he'd miss her. Sylvia and Elizabeth had clubbed together and, rather inappropriately, bought her a baby's layette. "We know it's going to be adopted …but you want to give it a good send off."

Emma stood at the bus stop to make the homeward journey for the last time. At first she didn't notice the two women gossiping alongside her in the queue, but then the fatter of the two turned to stare at her, casting a slow look up and down her pregnant body and ring-less hand. Raising her eyebrows disapprovingly, she nodded in affirmation to her friend. "Not married, you know."

The other woman threw a disdainful look at Emma and shook her head. "Common slut," she muttered, clear enough for Emma to hear. Emma felt rooted to the spot. A mixture of heartache, humiliation and anger swept over her. She felt unable to do or say anything. The bus pulled in at the stop and she didn't board. As the two women got on, she turned away sharply, clutching the baby's layette, and walked fiercely towards the city centre. Blindly she stormed onwards, her mind racing. Everything hurt too much. By the time she eventually got home, all she could recall was stuffing the baby's layette into a litter bin in town.

"Will it be okay?" asked John, rather unnerved by Emma's swollen naked body. She had changed shape since they'd last been together. Emma sat on the edge of Paul's bed, his room borrowed for a packet of twenty Embassy. John's hair had been bleached by the sun, his skin deeply tanned. Emma lusted for him, bowled over yet again with overwhelming physical infatuation. By comparison she felt fat and plain. She was hungry for reassurance as much as love.

"I should think so – the wee fella's had worse than you to put up with before now."

John moved towards her and squatted down, laying his face next to her stomach. Emma ran her hands over his blond hair, down his neck and over his firm brown shoulders. The baby kicked.

"Wow! Was that him?" Mesmerized, John tentatively caressed her stomach, feeling the shape, kissing her belly and murmuring softly. Suddenly he got up and moved away. "We can't do it. I can't do it now, with that... I don't know. It doesn't seem right," he sounded irritated, frustrated.

"Yes we can. Come on, John, please. I want you." Apprehensively, he moved towards her and lay down on the bed.

Afterwards, they lay there each with their own thoughts. John spoke first, recapping his plans. The following weekend he would go to Leeds, to sort out digs, come back for another week and then leave for good. Well, not for good – he promised to be back at weekends. He never asked Emma what she had been doing, didn't ask about her office job or if she'd been out at night, he didn't even ask whether she'd missed him. Neither did he check up on what books she'd read. Which was just as well because she hadn't read any.

She should have felt happy he was back, but she didn't. She wondered whether to suggest ending their relationship, not because she wanted to break up, but to force some emotional response from him. To see if he would cry or squeeze her tightly, begging her to stay.

Instead, she just lay there, listening, heavy hearted. "Did you go with anyone?" she risked.

John exhaled with punctuated jerks, trying to make smoke rings. He seemed more interested in doing that than answering her question. "Nah, never stayed in the same place long enough."

It wasn't quite the right answer.

"Katy and I went to the Casino to see Otis Redding while you were away."

"Yeah? Good for you. Was it good?"

"Brilliant! It was such a laugh dancing with blokes, you know – in this state!" Emma forced a dirty laugh.

"Oh yeah?" he turned to look at her, then stroked her cheek, "and you ask about me? I can see I'm going to have to keep an eye on you, you brazen hussy!" But it was said playfully – infuriatingly without a hint of distrust. Should she mention her idea of going to live in London? Perhaps that would make him jealous and he would realize how much he cared for her. Perhaps they would get married. Keep the baby… They lay curled round each other, silent and still, save for the restless little feet and elbows sandwiched between them.

Mrs Lacey put the stethoscope back in her medical bag and smiled. "Well, Baby appears to be alive and kicking and you seem fine, Emma. And how are you managing, Mrs Hargreaves?"

"Oh well, so so under the circumstances." They both gave each other what Emma called a "woman's look", making her feel like a child. Mrs Lacey nodded compassionately holding a long pause before turning to face her young patient. "And how are the antenatal classes going, Emma?"

"Okay, I guess. The woman who runs the class is a bit snooty with me, and most of the other mothers seem a lot older – but one girl's all right."

"What about your breathing? Are you practising that?"

"Yes," she lied.

"Good. We want an easy time, don't we? Keep it up!" With that, she smiled warmly and patted Emma's hair. "See you soon – but not too soon I hope!" And she left.

Emma's mum turned to her daughter and smiled, somewhat sadly. "Well, not long now, love," she said.

No. Not long now.

Chapter Four

The shops had started plugging Christmas. Emma waddled around the town gazing through shop windows. She had no intention of buying anything; she was just whiling away time before she met Katy.

"Hi!" Katy suddenly breezed up, breathless with face flushed from the icy winds. "The lecture was cancelled so we left early. How are you?"

"Hi! Fat, fed up and freezing."

"I see." They grinned at each other. "Best get mum-to-be a nice hot milk from the Coffee Shop, yeah?" Emma was happy to be with Katy. She was the only person in the world who she felt understood her.

"So, how long now?" asked Katy.

"Should be in a couple of days or so, but I reckon it'll be longer than that. Apparently the head's engaged and dropped – all good fun when you're bursting for a wee and sneeze! But the midwife reckons on more like next week."

"Jesus! Do you think you should be pottering around town like this? Shouldn't you be at home?"

"Oh I'm so BORED at home. The house stinks of paraffin because Mum's put all these heaters everywhere. Dad's still pretending nothing's going on and it's getting ridiculous. I don't really talk to him much anyway but now they're hardly talking to each other. Mum is so stressed it's as if she's on a knife edge and I'm just waiting, waiting, waiting…"

"I hate to be hard on you, but you should be bloody grateful. Your mum could have kicked you out – Jane MacKenzie's parents have."

"God, have they?"

"Yep. Gone to a mother and baby home in Gateshead."

"Oh no, poor thing. That's horrible. They say they make you nurse the baby, do everything, then when the new parents come they just say 'Right, pass it over'."

"I know. Rachael's heard from her and apparently they're scrubbing floors and being shouted at something rotten."

"That's awful. I've heard they're like prison camps. Poor Jane."

"So less of the old moaney bones, okay?"

"Okay miss." Emma touched her forelock submissively.

"Anyway, have you thought of any names for Baby?" Katy and Emma stood in the queue at the Coffee Shop. "One coffee and one hot milk, please," interjected Katy to the assistant.

"Thank you," they said in unison and found a table in the corner.

"Kind of yes and kind of no," said Emma. "I've always thought of him as Oliver, I don't know why – but he's not really mine to call anything, is he?"

"Oliver. That's nice, I like that. But what if 'he' is a girl?"

"Oh it's a boy all right."

"You can't know for sure..."

"I do." Emma had her elbows on the table, holding the mug of hot milk in both hands. She took a small, scalding sip and peered over the top of the mug through the steam, staring hard into Katy's eyes. "He's my best friend," she whispered confidentially, "We're in this together, Oliver and me. Against the world."

"Oh Emma..."

"I'm not too happy about your ankles. Bit puffy, aren't they?" Mrs Lacey was examining Emma on the bed. "I think it's time your wee fella made an appearance in this world. Perhaps we ought to persuade him."

"How?" asked Emma, a little worried. It was November 24th.

"We could try the OBE."

"What's that?"

"Let me go downstairs and have a word with your mother."

Emma looked around her bedroom. Just a couple of hard chairs and a sideboard remained with the bed in the middle of the room making the room look more like a surgical theatre. Emma lay on the rubber sheet now, naked from the waist down. She looked at the jug and bowl all ready. Ready for what? Emma shuddered. Her mother had been busy, working away to get everything sorted. Dad had been grumpy. The door opened and in walked Mrs Lacey and her mother.

"Okay Emma," smiled Mrs Lacey, bright and optimistic. "I've had a little chat with Mum and we're going for the OBE. Get all this behind you, yes?"

Emma just lay there, looking from one to the other. She suddenly felt frightened.

"Right, so up you get, pet. Make yourself decent and we'll start with the cocktail…"

The 'O' stood for oil – castor oil, a 2oz bottle of it, mixed with neat concentrate orange juice and water, stirred briskly and to be swallowed in one go. "Best take it over the sink, dear," Mrs Lacey had added. The 'B' was for bath, with the water so hot Emma's mother had to stay with her in case of fainting; followed finally with 'E' – a full, soapy enema. "That should do it!" laughed Mrs Lacey.

It didn't.

"I'm sorry, pet. If that's not going to do the trick, we're going to have to get you in somewhere. Whatever you've got in there, love, doesn't intend to budge!" Mrs Lacey looked compassionate, but helpless. She shrugged her shoulders and looked at Emma's mother. "We're going to have to get her admitted," she said softly, as if Emma shouldn't hear.

An hour later, Emma's father drove her to Parkview Maternity Hospital on the outskirts of Newcastle, the only home prepared to admit her, and even then – short stay only. Dad had been called home from work. Emma thought he'd go mad, refuse even, yet for all his stony silence, he obligingly co-operated. Maybe he was relieved she wasn't going to have the baby at home after all. Mum sat in the front next to Dad, Emma in the back clutching a small bag with night clothes and baby clothes. Apart from her parents vaguely discussing directions, no-one spoke. Emma stared through the windows, idly glancing at the passing familiar scenery. She caught a faint smell of her father's Imperial Leather aftershave and for a second her senses carried her back to being a little girl sitting on his knee. The same smell. Now they were so distant they hardly knew each other.

"Left at the next junction, dear," said Kathleen. She turned round to face her daughter, "Okay love?"

Emma smiled politely. "Yes thanks, Mum." She was now focused on getting on with things and wanted to be alone – well, alone with Oliver. It was strange, because she didn't really know how she was feeling. For nine months, she had been a vessel for carrying what, in effect, was someone else's child. Her pregnancy hadn't altogether felt hers and now the culmination of other people's arrangements was imminent. She had rarely allowed herself much thought to how she might feel after the birth. There was a secret love affair between Oliver and herself, almost a forbidden intimacy; yet now the reality of touching, smelling, owning – albeit temporarily – this small human life felt unnerving. Her mother's face was full of anguish, pity, fear even. Emma didn't want that. She was suddenly too busy herself to handle her mum's concern, however well intentioned.

The car pulled up the drive of Parkfield Maternity Home.

"Thanks, both of you. I mean it. You can just drop me off here."

"Are you sure, dear? We'll come in if you want," said Mum.

"No. Really, I'd prefer to just get on with it." Emma got out the car and smiled at both of them, genuinely grateful and sorry for what she was putting them through. Kathleen looked lost, and Emma noticed her dad briefly pat her mum's shoulder before winding down the window.

"We'll ring the hospital in a while," he grunted uncomfortably, offering an assertive nod as if "things would be taken care of now". Then he turned the car round and they drove away.

C'mon kiddar, Emma said to herself. Here goes…

Parkview Maternity Hospital would have provided a happy stay in more favourable circumstances, but the nurses treated Emma like a loose tart. A brusque internal examination followed by a minor surgical procedure had Emma gushing warm water from between her legs. Embarrassed and sorry, she murmured apologies. She thought she had wet herself.

"I've broken your waters," said the nurse. No smile. No warmth. Emma was then wheeled to a delivery room and left unattended, being told to pull the alarm cord when absolutely necessary.

"When will that be?"

"You'll know."

After two hours, Emma was aware that her contractions were coming every fifteen minutes but they were not painful. For all the hostile attitude towards her, she didn't feel frightened or lonely. She wasn't alone. She had her baby inside her, they were in this together. But again, a conflict of emotion stirred within her. Yes, they were in it together – and yet, he wasn't hers. Poor baby. Defenceless. It seemed to bring them closer together. What a muddle.

At one time, a nurse popped her head round the door and grinned. "I shouldn't be doing this," she whispered, casting a furtive look over her shoulder, "but there's some pea soup for supper. Did you want some?"

Emma was elated by this friendly act of kindness and said "Yes, please." Within minutes, the young nurse came back again with a bowl of steaming hot soup. She winked at Emma and promised to return shortly to take the bowl away.

From eleven pm onwards Emma was having increasingly strong contractions, each one lasting several minutes. She wondered whether to call for help, wanting to leave it as long as possible for fear of further reprisal. Suddenly, a violent and powerful downward pressure hardened her stomach like rock and she could not stop herself bearing down. Panting and sweaty and terrified her body was about to split open, she reached out her hand and pulled the cord.

Two midwives came into delivery room, briefly looked between Emma's legs and immediately busied themselves for the birth. Efficient and indifferent, they issued reassurance, and instructions. "Pant a bit, that's it – hold it. Good girl, relax – take it easy. And again, push when I say so, that's it – good girl, come on…"

Emma panted and pushed, slotting in gulps of air between what now seemed continuous contractions.

"What a lovely mop of blond hair! Easy does it, yes – and again, here it comes!"

Just as Emma knew she was about to die…whoosh! The head, followed by the easier slither of tiny shoulders and then all of him, warm, wet and wrinkly, making a faint sound, like an old creaking gate. Emma raised her head and saw him lying there, so small – pink limbs flaying, face screwed up, a fat umbilical cord still bonding her to him. One of the midwives severed their tie and attached a tiny clip to his tummy. She smiled at Emma and picked him up in a blanket. Just then he filled his tiny lungs and let out a huge cry.

"Is he okay?" Emma's voice sounded thin and exhausted.

"Perfect."

Hey presto. One son. It was over. A perfect baby boy. It was 11.45pm. The midwife holding Emma's baby briefly tilted the little bundle for her to see, she eased her frame up on one shaky elbow to look at him and was suddenly overcome by the fact of his existence.

"Hello Oliver. Welcome to the world." Then she flopped back down with a huge grin across her face.

One of the nurses attended to Oliver and took him to the nursery. After a little while, Emma was ready to be wheeled back to the ward. Another new mum lay in a bed opposite. "Hi," she whispered. "Okay?"

"Yes," boasted Emma, feeling like the only woman ever to have given birth. "I've had a son! A beautiful baby boy!"

A sister walked up to Emma and leaned over her bed glaring at her. "Shut up. Let her get some sleep."

The next morning, two ambulance men stood at the entrance to the ward; one held a baby.

"*Miss Hargreaves?*" savoured the Ward Sister, addressing Emma. Emma blinked, half asleep. "Come on. Time for you to go." Opening her eyes and quickly resuming consciousness Emma focused on the small bundle held by the man. Easing herself slowly over the side of the bed, she slipped on her dressing gown with the aid of the unencumbered ambulance man and stood on two wobbly legs.

"Are you all right, love?" he asked kindly, but Emma's eyes were riveted to the other man – the one with the bundle.

"Yes thanks, I – I'm fine. Please…?" She stretched out her arms. Her baby was given to her as she was swivelled into a waiting wheelchair. Nothing else registered. There was the journey home, a delicate waddle to the front door and a welcome from her mum. But Emma was spellbound with little Oliver. Perfect in every detail: tiny fingers, little nose, mop of blond hair, smelling so sweet, breathing, warm, a life…a life she and John had made between them. Their baby. She loved him. Loved him desperately, with a savage maternal depth she could never have imagined.

John had been thinking of Emma for days. November 13th the baby had been due, hadn't it? The last time he'd phoned, two days ago, she still hadn't had it. Now it was the 24th. Should he phone again? Mrs Hargreaves' attitude towards him put him off calling, but Emma was on his mind. He was starting to find her late pregnancy a bit repulsive and was looking forward to seeing her slim again. Maybe too, once it was all behind her, she'd perk up a bit. She seemed so weepy and insecure.

"Yes, she's here. A boy. Yes, they're both well. Did you want to speak to her? Oh, very well. Yes, I'll tell her. Yes, yes. Thank you. Bye." Emma's mother replaced the receiver.

"That was John," she said turning to Emma who was lying on the settee. "He couldn't stay on the phone for long as he was calling from Leeds and had no more money, but he'll be coming to see you tomorrow. At about six o'clock." Emma sensed her mother's hostility; John was not welcome, but it was inappropriate to refuse to let him come and see his own son.

"You can't just pick him up, John, he's fast asleep."

John was peering into the borrowed carrycot next to Emma's bed. Emma was resting on top of the eiderdown. The room was less bare than before, the furniture had been brought back – clothes, magazines and make-up, made it much more comfortable. A paraffin heater stood in the corner giving off as much pungent odour as heat.

"Come here, little son," said John disregarding Emma and plucking the small baby from his cot. "Let's have a look at you." To Emma's surprise, John sat on the edge of the bed, cradling their baby, rocking him gently, talking softly and marvelling at his miniature perfection. "Look at these fingers!" He held the tiny hand and gently uncurled it. "He's even got little nails – look at this, on his little finger!"

Emma looked and smiled. She understood. But it was a side of John she had never seen before, and rather unexpected. He sat there, transfixed, touching little bits of his body, his nose, his ears, lifting up his nightdress like a child might explore a new doll, cupping his large hand over tiny knees, running a finger down his small chest, loving, cuddling their baby, oblivious to everything – including Emma. Oliver slept on, seeming content and secure in his father's arms. Eventually John very tenderly put him down, laying him down and arranging the bedding around him. He smiled at Emma, his blue eyes alive with wonder.

"And you?" John asked quietly.

"Fine. Everything went okay in the end. They were a bit snooty at the hospital though."

John nodded and fell silent for a while.

"Steve Walters is having a party on Sunday. Just a few friends round at his house while his parents are away. Any chance of you coming?"

"Oh, I don't know John. I had a baby on Thursday you know!"

John grinned. "Yeah, I know. Just thought I'd ask. In a way, I thought it would be good for you, for us – you know, like old times."

"Mmm. Maybe I could if I took it dead easy. I'll ask Mum later."

She felt close to John now, bonded through their joint creation, even though their son was going to be adopted. They could share this moment, hold it in memory for life. And they had each other. They would always have each other.

"Oh Emma! You've only just given birth – surely you can't possibly want to go to a party?"

"I wouldn't stay late or do anything. Just sit and be there."

Kathleen felt confused and tired. Most of the time the carrycot and baby were with her, downstairs. She was sleeping with the baby, feeding him, changing him, to stop Emma making a close bond with her son. She agreed so as to avoid argument. "But you must wrap up well, wear several pairs of knickers and do walk about as little as possible. You must have a taxi there and back – John must promise me this. And NO dancing!"

"Thanks Mum!"

Perhaps it wouldn't be such a bad thing, reflected Emma's mother. Emma had missed a year of being young. Physically she seemed amazingly well, and it might make things easier for her when the baby was gone. Kathleen's heart lurched.

That night, Emma lay in bed dreaming about the party. What should she wear? Her tummy had gone quite flat straight away, but her breasts were colossal – and leaking. She was taking pills to dry up her milk, but it was proving a slow and uncomfortable process. The purple mini skirt would fit, no problem – but the skinny rib polo neck jumper would have to be a no no. Still, she had a great store of false eyelashes and a new brown blusher to give the hollow cheeks look… Suddenly, Emma caught her breath and went rigid. Downstairs she heard a tiny cry, like the creak of an old gate, then the low rumble of movement as her mother tended the baby.

The cry did something to her. She wasn't sure what, but it felt heavy, like a dead weight lying within her. She lay there motionless, trying to capture every sound, straining to hear her baby's whimper. Milk trickled out of her nipples. She touched her breasts, they were rock hard, she felt some fluid run onto her finger and put it to her lips. It tasted sweet, weak, warm. Emma just lay flat on her back, staring into darkness, listening to Oliver's cry. The soft distant muffle of her mum's voice, inaudible through the walls, like a woolly drone, then more shuffling, creaking, whispering – and finally, silence. Emma's heart pounded against her chest, and yet there was a strange absence of emotion – just a heavy emptiness.

Oliver was due to be collected at about eleven am on Monday 5th December. He was ready, in his carrycot in the kitchen, all wrapped up in a little blue knitted cardigan, hat and bootees. Her dad was at work; her mum was upstairs making the beds. Emma was just hanging around drifting from room to room. She sat down in the front room. She got up. She didn't know whether to hold Oliver one more time or not. She found herself in the kitchen.

She felt strange; detached yet dull, as if her senses were on hold. Slowly, she scooped the swaddled bundle from his cot and held him close to her. Just holding him there made her breasts tingle. He smelt sweet, a tiny drop of moisture glistened on his lips. Softly, she licked his mouth, then scattered his tiny face with kisses, furrowing into him, smothering his nose and cheeks with hers. Her nose buried into his warmth and she drew his baby fragrance into her, his small breaths blanketed with hers. Nothing mattered but this moment. She held him there, their faces pressed together.

He was a part of her. They were one. She couldn't get close enough and she held him more tightly. Oliver creaked and twitched a bit.

"Sssh Baby, it's only me." Emma released her arms a little, softened the pressure on his body from her face. She flinched. A feeling of pain filled the void momentarily, but then whatever it was was gone again. "Love you, babe. I'll find you again one day. Promise." She kissed the end of his nose and put him back in his carrycot. Then she took herself into the front room and sat down staring at the wall.

Time passed. It could have been two hours or ten minutes. The doorbell rang. Emma's mum opened the door. Emma could hear voices in the hall. Footsteps receded into the kitchen – and back again. She could hear mutterings, assurances, farewells.

The door closed.

The door closed and he was gone.

She heard her mother make a strange sound. Emma still sat there staring at the wall. The house seemed empty. She didn't cry.

After a while, she got up and went into the kitchen. Her mother was washing pots at the sink. Emma poured herself a glass of milk. Neither of them said anything. It was over.

Chapter Five

Katy sipped her coffee pensively. She sat facing Emma at the same quayside coffee bar where she and Emma had first met John and Jeffrey seventeen months before. Emma ran her finger round the brim of her cup, almost nervously. There was a hollow look in her eyes.

"But what will you do? Where will you live? You can't just go like that, surely?"

"Remember Alan Swinton from school? I saw him at Steve's party a couple of weeks ago, he'd come up from London. He has a place in Putney now. I can stay there while I get somewhere of my own. He said I'm welcome."

"What about work?"

"There'll be no problem, honest. They have employment agencies and accommodation agencies on virtually every street corner. Hey! You sound as bad as Mum!"

Katy grinned. "Soz God. But what about me? I'll miss you."

"It's London I'm going to – not the moon. When I'm all sorted you can come and stay with me. We can get a place together when you've finished college!" Emma tilted back in her chair, laughing, drumming her fingers on the table. Her nails were badly bitten. Katy had never noticed that before.

"What does John say?"

"I kind of haven't told him yet. I hinted that I fancied living in London, but either he doesn't believe me or wasn't listening. We're not so good again at the moment." Emma let her chair relax, stopped drumming her fingers and looked into Katy's eyes to see if she was really attentive. "I found a letter…it fell out of his jacket pocket. Dated last August but he never sent it. To some girl in Malmo, you know – from when he went round Europe with his friends. Anyway, it said: 'don't worry, I'll either come over or send some money'."

"So?" asked Katy, not registering.

"So he fucked a girl in Sweden and got her pregnant, right?"

"Oh God no! Oh Emma, I'm sorry. Are you sure? Does John know you found the letter?"

"You bet. I threw my drink into his face and said 'What's this?' waving it under his nose. He said I'd jumped to conclusions, got it all wrong, that it wasn't as I thought – but he didn't deny it either."

"Bloody hell. So what happened?"

"I don't know. I don't think he ever got in touch with her. Maybe she had an abortion, or she wasn't pregnant in the end."

"Perhaps a fresh start would do you good." Katy rested her hand on top of Emma's and patted it. They held each other's gaze and Katy sensed her friend felt deserted. She wondered if losing Oliver had disturbed Emma; she hadn't spoken of him since he'd gone. Perhaps it would be unwise to mention it.

"Anyway," resumed Emma, "I'm pissed off at home, too. I've got to get out, got to get away. I'm sick of it here. Pathetic Northern hell hole. Everyone's so petty minded."

"What, and me?"

"No. You're all right. It's all the others." Emma grinned, but it was an agitated grin. Katy returned her smile but she felt uncomfortable. Emma seemed so restless, aggressive even. It was unnerving.

Emma knew that if she didn't get a move on, it would have to be George Green & Co again. The atmosphere at home was uncomfortable to say the least. Her father seemed particularly bad tempered; Emma never had felt close to him – well, not since she'd been a very little girl. She'd been the apple of his eye then. But they'd grown apart. Mum was slightly more tolerable, but none of them ever really talked together. Now her parents were at each other's throats and Emma sensed herself to be the cause of it.

Emma's mother was aware that she was restless but said nothing. It seemed to her that her daughter was making it unpleasant for everyone at home. John was not around so much these days and although in the past, nothing would have pleased her more, she now wished the two of them were closer. It might have made Emma more bearable. Kathleen herself was unwell, suffering from stomach problems, and desperately wanted peace and quiet around her. Jack seemed to be sick and tired of them both.

When Emma announced she was finally leaving, her mother received the news with mixed feelings. Her father said nothing and carried on as usual. Emma had sorted through her clothes, selected the bare essentials and been in touch with Alan. Her mother had allowed her daughter access to savings of £32.18 left over from her grandfather's will, and added £2.10 from her own housekeeping – as much to relieve feelings of guilt as give financial security. She thought perhaps it improper that they allow Emma to leave home for London at such a young age, to such a big city so far away. How on earth would Emma cope? She had only been to London once as a child. And yet, she desperately needed Emma to go. For her and Jack's sake.

"Why?" John sounded scared, weak. Emma thought briefly of all the times she had wanted to squeeze emotion out of him to satisfy her own insecurity – and now, she didn't want it. Didn't need it. Did she?

They lay together on top of Paul's bed, silent for the moment, a heavy sadness weighing them both down.

"Why London?"

"Because that's where's it's all happening. I need to have some life, John. I need to move on, leave the past behind."

"But you don't have to end it, end us…"

"Things have changed. You've got Leeds, you've got your life there. And you know you like your independence." Emma's voice softly but determinedly retaliated, "Now I want mine."

"You mean the girl from Malmo? Oh she was nothing, Emma. Don't screw us up because of that."

"It's not just that. It's everything. I need to get away and do my own thing."

"But why London? What will you do? It's such a hard, fast city Emma, you're not used to that. You'll get taken advantage of. Some slimy bastard will worm his way into your knickers. You don't know what men are like."

"Oh, don't I?"

"Not really. You're so naive. You'll just get taken for a ride."

"You're just jealous."

John sighed. He lay on his back, hands behind his head, staring at the ceiling. "Anyway, I don't want to lose you. We've only just got going again. I know it's been difficult, especially for you…with everything." He didn't mention the baby. Emma hadn't shown any reaction to Oliver's going and he thought it safer not to say anything himself. Make matters worse.

"Anyway, I'm going. I've got it all sorted. First of all, I'm staying with Alan in Putney, then I'll find my own pad." Inside, Emma was wavering. John's emotional plea was nibbling at her cold exterior, and yet she was enjoying hurting him.

"I don't want you to go."

"I'll keep in touch…" Emma had control. She was playing with him, for once she held the power. The tension was building between them. She delighted in her new role and twisted the knife in further. "I need to meet more men. Gain some experience, see more of the world." He deserved this, but quite why, she wasn't sure.

John lay silent. Sulking. He suddenly turned to Emma and squeezed her so tightly she could hardly breathe. "It's only you that matters to me. Do you understand? Don't end it. Go to London – do your 'own thing' if you have to, but don't end it."

Emma didn't resist. They lay together, arms and legs around each other. Then Emma felt a catch in his breathing. Dampness from his lashes brushed her cheek. She needed this. Needed to make him feel abandoned, bereft. It felt like revenge, it felt slightly insane. Anger swirled around inside her, merging with satisfaction and desire.

"Please, Emma…" he smothered her wet cheeks with his kisses.

Strangely appeased, Emma felt the tension in her snap. She tightened her grip on him, sucking the tears from his face as they rocked together, entwined; both weeping, for different reasons, for the same reasons, for themselves, for each other, for their lost baby.

The hustle and bustle of St Pancras overwhelmed Emma. She stood on the platform with one suitcase, a holdall and a shoulder bag draped across her shoulders. How the hell did one get to Putney from St Pancras? Everyone moved so quickly, so purposefully: commuters, shoppers, travellers.

A tube. That's what she needed to do, catch a tube. How? She fell in with the flow and soon found herself confronted with a huge sign saying London Underground. Emma stared at a map of the underground, totally confused, searching for "Putney". She had only been to London once in her life, as a small child with her family for a day trip. A middle-aged woman stood next to Emma, also looking at the map.

"Excuse me, please," said Emma, "where's Putney?"

The woman smiled and pointed to it on the map, miles away from St Pancras. "You want the Victoria line to Victoria, then change to the District line for Putney. That's it, there."

Emma reached Alan Swinton's place two hours later; a semi-detached house in an ordinary suburban district – not at all like the London she'd imagined.

"Hi!" greeted Alan. "You made it."

"Just," puffed Emma, dumping her things in the hall. She looked around, empty beer bottles littered the floor, a pile of dirty washing lay at the bottom of the stairs, a telephone stood on a table next to a mouldy cup and over-full ash tray. The house smelled of beer, sweat and stale fish and chips.

"Thanks for letting me stay over," lied Emma, swallowing her nausea. "I should be able to get a place of my own within a day or two." (Please God.)

"No problem. No hurry. Mike and I are happy for you to kip on the floor as long as you want."

Kipping on the floor meant cushions from the settee and a dirty old blanket. That night, Emma felt a million miles from home; lonely and disconnected. She thought of John, of their last emotional meeting in Paul's bedsit and her promise of keeping in touch, and wanted to have him lying next to her. She thought of her mum, tears welling up in her eyes. The night was long, cold and uncomfortable. She would leave first thing in the morning.

Earls Court Road was much more like the London she'd imagined. It had taken over an hour to get there from Putney; both Alan and Mike had seemed quite put out that she'd wanted to leave so soon, but no way was Emma staying another night.

"Just a single room for one?" questioned the man the other side of the desk. He flipped open a huge file. "What area?"

"I don't mind really. Maybe around here."

"There are quite a few bedsits, but we'd need a month's rent up front. Have you got a job?" He was looking hard at Emma. Was she a runaway?

"Not yet...that's next on my list."

"Have your parents given you an allowance? Presuming, that is, they know you're here?"

"Yes. They know." Emma felt they'd been glad to see the back of her, although she knew her mum worried. "And I have just under £32."

"Hmm. That sounds reasonable. Bedsits are generally around £5 a week, so a month in advance, you're looking at £20. But you will need a job. Nowhere will take you on unemployed. I suggest you go down the road to Blakes Employment Agency, fix yourself up with something and come back later."

"Age?"

"Nineteen." She wasn't quite, but nearly.

"Done any shop work before?"

"Well, no. But I know I could do it."

The woman filled in a card with some details and passed it to Emma while dialing a telephone number. A brief telephone conversation was exchanged, the woman nodding affirmatively at Emma in the process. She put down the receiver and smiled at Emma. "Right. Miss Selfridge in Oxford Street. Report there at nine in the morning – the side entrance is in Orchard Street. You need to see a Miss Putnam and take that card, explaining you're from the agency. Okay?"

Whoopie! chuckled Emma to herself and almost skipped back to the accommodation agency. By mid-afternoon, she had a bedsit in Gloucester Road with a job starting the next day. She felt capable and independent and bought herself a packet of ten No.6 cigarettes as a special treat. She rarely smoked, sneaking the occasional drag from John, but now she was a single girl in London. Adult. She deserved a packet of cigarettes.

The journey from Gloucester Road to Selfridges involved changing tubes at Nottinghill Gate and getting off at Marble Arch. Emma was mesmerized – now *this* was London! The train was full of commuters, weirdos, young people, beautiful people, all avoiding eye contact, locked into a world of their own, reading papers, sleeping, staring into space.

She'd had a sleepless night in her new bedsit with doors banging, others in the house shouting and coughing, the strangeness of four new walls – but it had been better than staying with Alan and Mike. She had cooked beans on toast whilst mentally buying a couple of posters to stick on the wall. Still feeling resilient she alighted at Marble Arch and bustling with the crowds, soon found herself at the side entrance to Selfridges.

"I'm looking for a Miss Putnam in the Miss Selfridge department…" Emma approached a strikingly attractive girl, about her own age. She had abrupt, short spikey dyed black hair and black lines painted on her cheek as lower lashes. She looks like Julie Driscoll, drooled Emma.

"Sure, come with me!" The girl breezed through the store, empty save for employees and security officials, tossing questions back to Emma who followed in hot pursuit. "Your first day? I'm Sheena, on knitwear in Miss Selfridge. Not from round here, are you?"

"Yes, no. My first day – from Newcastle actually. I'm Emma." Emma wanted to stay with Sheena forever. She could be her first friend, a real London friend.

"Here we are," beamed Sheena, "Miss Putnam's fab, just like one of us. See you for ciggies and coffee later, maybe!" And she left Emma outside an office with the words 'MISS PUTNAM. DEPARTMENTAL MANAGERESS' on the door. Emma knocked.

"Come in."

She entered to face a pretty, smiling woman, about thirty, in high fashion clothes and long, Jean Shrimpton styled hair. Emma handed Miss Putnam the card from the Agency. After a few administrative details were taken, she was led back into the store and put under the protective supervision of Sheena on the knitwear counter.

After three weeks, Sheena and Emma had become close friends. Sheena shared a flat with a girl in Brunswick Gardens, Kensington. The girl was leaving. Did Emma want to move in? You bet!

Emma had been in touch with John, Katy and her parents, yet felt reluctant to divulge her address in Gloucester Road as it had soon become apparent she wasn't staying. The bedsit had proved to be a slum with others in the house being drug addicts, alcoholics or downright bums. The residential communal phone precluded privacy and call boxes were invariably out of order. John was without phone access most of the time anyway. She'd managed to call him once, through Paul, but it had seemed years since they'd known each other. Also, talking to John had left Emma vengeful again; depressed.

One evening, just after she and Sheena had planned her moving in date, Emma phoned Katy from a telephone kiosk at Marble Arch tube station. Feeling elated and confident, she wanted to boast of her improved status and invite Katy to come down one weekend to her new place.

"Really, it's great here!" laughed Emma, "Sheena is a fab friend and I'm moving in with her at the weekend. It's a really groovy pad, so neat – psychedellic posters on the wall – honest Kate you'd love it, it is so cool!" Emma was working on her speech and the words she used.

"Yes, I'd like that. You sound as if you're having a good time…"

"Yah, great! How's everyone back in Newcastle?"

"Oh much the same. One girl has dropped out of the course, Sue Holman – don't know if you know her? Oh yes! Gossip or what, do you remember Jane MacKenzie? The one who went to the mother and baby home in Gateshead?"

Emma went cold. Did she want to hear this?

"Well, " continued Katy, "she's refused to let the baby go. Caused havoc apparently, screamed the place down when they tried to take him away and now she's insisting she keeps him and stuff authority. God knows what she'll do because her parents won't have her back unless she gives the baby up – and she'll never find work now…"

Emma's throat went dry. Her thoughts crashed chaotically. Something was wrong, like a twisted inside out feeling. She held the receiver limply for a moment. Then the shutters came down or the barriers up. Whatever.

All that remained was a heavy nauseous feeling. Briefly she noticed one of her fingers was bleeding; she must have bitten the nail too far down.

"Are you still there, Emma?"

"Er, yeah, sure… I'm out of change, Katy. I'll ring again soon."

The smell reminded Emma of compost or dry burning leaves. Sheena sat crossed legged on the floor, eyes closed, inhaling the fat joint and breathing deeply, holding the smoke in her lungs for several seconds before exhaling, shaking her head as a reaction to its effect. Emma watched, keen to learn. Rizla cigarette papers littered the floor, a stolen pub ashtray lay between them. She passed the joint to Emma. Gingerly, Emma sucked. It tasted herbal, woody, but it felt like a normal cigarette. She drew in a little harder until her head went dizzy and light. A triumphant feeling of well being coursed through her – was it the cannabis or relief at surviving her first, real drag?

"Good stuff, yeah?" asked Sheena, smiling.

"Wow!" nodded Emma.

Sheena swayed to Donovan's *Mellow Yellow* on the record player, humming softly. She had tied an Indian scarf around her hair, the long ends falling down the side of her face, brushing her cheeks as she rocked gently from side to side.

Emma wondered if she felt sick and passed the joint back to Sheena. The darkened room now seemed to be glowing, flickering flames from candles in old wine bottles made shadowy patterns on the walls. A sheet of tie-dyed muslin pinned on the door wafted in the slight breeze from a crack in the dirty window. Emma's sense perceptions seemed exaggerated; everything had meaning.

No, she didn't feel sick. She felt good. Emma stood up and began dancing dreamily around the room to the music, then Sheena started moving with Emma, both singing at the top of their voices: "They call me mella yella!" They passed the joint from one to the other, laughing, arms flaying, heads swinging from side to side – Emma's soft straight hair, now long, kept falling across her face. She was happy, so happy. Right now, life was happy, life was love. Love was life. That was all that mattered. Sheena was wonderful, so mature. And now she, too, was beginning to understand what it was all about. The room began to spin. The posters on the wall danced around with them. The candles were happy. Happiness was spinning.

"Oh wow – this is cool!" they slurred in unison.

Emma and Sheena enjoyed working at Miss Selfridge but fantasized about having a stall on the Kensington Flea Market one day. A couple of friends of theirs, Maxine and Clive, rented a small space in the complex and were basking in a lucrative trade selling Indian cheesecloth shirts, long, cotton wrap-around skirts and American Indian beads. A mood of free love pervaded their young, idealized thinking – and it was trendy just to be happy. Emma loved hanging around the market with Sheena, drifting from stall to stall, smiling and saying "Hi man," to everyone.

That night at their flat, Sheena and Emma hung a large purple paper lightshade they had just bought from the market around the coloured bulb in the centre of the living room. The softened light gave a smokey hue, and as the paper shade twisted and turned, so the light moved, sliding round the walls.

"Wow – just fab!" enthused Emma, then quietly added as an after-thought, "I wonder what John would think if he could see this pad."

She had told Sheena all about their relationship, but not about the baby. They told each other everything – but not that. It was as if she had cut that right out of her life. It wasn't that she was keeping it a secret, but it was as if that part of her no longer existed. Almost as though it had never happened.

"Hey, ring him Emma, go on! It would be really cool to meet this guy."

"Uh huh, I don't know Sheena. Like I don't really know whether we're in a relationship or not. It's kind of difficult."

"Well, just let whatever happens, happen. Invite him down."

"Mmm." Emma nibbled her fingernail pensively, then lit a cigarette. Yes, she would like John to see her new pad, meet her hippie flatmate and their friends. She wanted him to be intimidated by her cultivated speech, her smoking pot, her high fashion gear and the cool London scene she was part of.

"Oh go on, Emma. It would be really cool!" Sheena turned the record over. The flip side was Paul McCartney singing *We Can Work It Out.*

"Sure, that would be great," said John on the other end of the phone. "I finish for the summer in a couple of weeks so maybe I can get work down there and stay awhile?"

"That would be really cool." Neither of them quite knew what the invite meant. It had been six months since they'd last been together, with little communication after that. A kind of limbo. They were both apprehensive but excited. By the time Sheena came in, she had taken two aspirin for a tension headache.

"Does he sleep with me or not?" Emma asked Sheena.

"Do you want him too?"

"I don't know. Like he's like a stranger now, it's been so long…and yet after all we've been through, it seems silly putting him up on the settee."

"Well perhaps you'd better get yourself on the pill. You don't want to get pregnant – that would bugger everything up for sure."

No, she wouldn't want to get pregnant.

"Can you get it if you're not married?"

"Not usually," Sheena said, "but this is London – and the local doctor round here is really groovy. If you tell him you're engaged and that you have really bad periods I'm sure he'll be okay about it."

Chapter Six

Emma went to meet John at St Pancras.

"Hi," she grinned, embarrassed and suddenly shy. He looked older, more rugged, his hair was longer and very blond against his tan – a handsome stranger. Mysterious but known too; new, exciting and available.

"Hi. You seem, er, kind of different," shrugged John, as nonplussed as she was. Emma looked way out, wearing a cheesecloth shirt, rows of beads around her neck and wide thin cotton flares. Her hair was parted in the middle and fell like a sheet over her shoulders. Her eyes drooped with the weight of false eyelashes. They didn't touch each other.

"You best lead the way," said John, straightening his back and arranging the rucksack more comfortably. They walked together, talking politely until they finally reached Brunswick Gardens. Emma took out her key and opened the door. Immediately, there was a smell of incense sticks and hash. John raised his eyebrows fractionally and threw Emma a quizzical look.

"It's different here, you know," she said.

Sheena threw her arms open and gave John a warm, uninhibited hug. She wore a loose kaftan, an Indian scarf plaited round her head and dark, smudgy, smouldering eye makeup. "Oh wow – fab! You must be John, I've heard so much about you!" John was clearly delighted with her embrace but not exactly comfortable. "Smoke?" she proffered the stub of her joint.

"Thanks, but I'll stick to nicotine." He dropped his rucksack and looked around.

"Would you like a cup of tea?" asked Emma.

"Please." John followed her into the kitchen. "Weird!" he whispered to Emma.

"What's weird?"

"She is," he nodded to the back room.

"Sheena? Nah – she's groovy. A real good friend."

John silenced his thoughts and wondered whether he would be sleeping with Emma that night. She seemed a stranger, totally different from the old Emma, but rather exciting.

"So how's Leeds? And Newcastle?"

They stood in the kitchen supping tea.

"Okay. And London?"

"Oh really fab. Have you seen Katy?"

"Not for a couple of months. I've stayed mainly in Leeds. She's not been down then?"

"Nah, like I really would love to see her, it's been so long, but I don't know, life seems so hectic and I just haven't got in touch with her. It's really fab here," added Emma.

John smiled. Emma winced slightly deep inside. For a second, something hurt. "You look good," he said and their eyes locked in mutual attraction. Emma flushed, John raised one eyebrow seductively. Feelings were coming back. He touched her hair, excited by her memory, wanting to have her again.

"When I saw you at St Pancras it was like I didn't know you, you looked so different," admitted John, relaxed now and sexually satisfied. "But I guess you're still my Emma." He ruffled her hair affectionately.

But Emma felt wrong. She lay back, silent. It was like a knot, all tangled up. John ran his finger down her nose, and pressed the little button end like a doorbell. She screwed up her face.

"Okay?" he asked.

"Yeah, sure."

It was as if by making love she had been drawn into a black box. Perhaps she didn't love him. But did that matter? A tight band wound itself round Emma's head and her tummy hurt.

Sheena adored John and he grew to find her loveable and entertaining. He also got on well with Maxine and Clive, spending daytime hours helping them at the market while the two girls worked at Miss Selfridge. In the evenings sometimes the five of them would gather round at Brunswick Gardens to smoke pot and listen to music. John joined in, albeit reservedly. He was becoming troubled with Emma's attitude towards him. He sensed an undercurrent of negative feelings from her whenever he said or did anything. She always appeared agitated the minute he was around, chain smoking and biting her nails to the quick. He'd been staying there nearly three weeks, maybe it was time for him to go.

"Do you want me to leave?" he asked her one afternoon when they had the flat to themselves.

"I don't know what I want."

"What's up? If it's anything I've said or done, just tell me."

Emma looked at John standing there – intelligent, level headed, coping. "God, I hate you!"

"Why? What have I done? Just tell me what I've done!"

Emma didn't know. She wanted him to rush over and hug her. "You just make me mad. I really think it's over now."

"If that's what you want… I would just like to understand you a bit more, that's all."

"How can you? You're just so arrogant, insensitive, dominating."

"Me insensitive? And you're up and down like a bloody yo-yo. I never know what's coming next!"

"Well there you are then. You'll be pleased to go. Give you some freedom. Be nice for you to get away from me." Emma's heart felt as if it was breaking.

John walked about the room, shaking his head in defeat. If he was thinking about the baby he didn't dare bring the subject up.

She felt the grip of black depression tighten, unable to control its growing power; it seemed to possess her – bitter, scary. "Yeah, maybe you had better go." That was the last thing she wanted. A voice inside her was screaming "Help me! Make me better!"

John skulked off to the bedroom and started to gather his belongings, shoving them into his rucksack. "I don't know what's up with you, you're screwing us up, Emma."

"Just get out! Get out! GET OUT!" Emma was shouting. Why was she shouting? She wanted him desperately. If only he would take her by the shoulders, shake her, tell her he loved her. But she was unlovable. She was driving him away.

"Okay, I'm, going." He picked up his bag and headed towards the door.

They held their gaze but Emma was possessed, hard and resolute. "Fuck off," she spat. Oh, please don't go...

He walked into the hall, opened the door and stared helplessly at her. Then he turned, walked out and closed the door behind him.

The door closed. He was gone.

Emma ran screaming into the kitchen. "He's gone! He's gone! Oh my God, what have I done?" She picked up a plate from the draining board and dropped it onto the floor, watching the pieces crash and scatter. And then she picked up another plate and did the same. She knew she was insane. She was so full of anger it was driving her crazy.

Suddenly, Emma was aware of a presence and looked up to see Sheena staring at her, mouth agape. "What on earth's happened?" she asked, her eyes cast onto the smashed crockery all over the kitchen floor.

"John's gone."

"Oh no. Why?"

"I told him to." Emma flopped down onto a chair, her temper subsiding, her energy drained.

"What's the matter, Emma?" Sheena sat down next to Emma at the kitchen table. Emma held her head in her hands, her face contorted with pain.

"He let them... John let them take my b..." choking on her own words, gulping for air yet nearer to panic than tears. "It's just finished."

"I'm sorry." Sheena was concerned by her friend's violence and erratic behaviour. "Do you want to talk?"

Yes. No. Yes. No.

"No."

Emma had the urge to run away. Perhaps it was time to move on again. Forget John. And now Sheena had got perilously close to...this madness within her. She was mad. She was sick, mentally sick. Yes. She must move on. Sheena was making her crazy, too.

Sheena had been devastated but Emma remained unreasonable and unapproachable. No, it was nothing personal. No, she hadn't done anything wrong. Yes, of course they would stay friends. Emma also handed in her notice at work. Yes, she had been happy there. No, she hadn't got another job as yet. Wriggle wriggle, squirm squirm. Emma desperately wanted space and privacy. She would find a bedsit, get another job where no-one knew her, be anonymous, start again.

21 Cromwell Road was a large, decrepit palisaded terraced house. Emma was in the basement; the window, sunk below the pavement, had iron bars – looking out and up, just the feet of passers-by could be seen. Her room was a small bedsit with basic cooking facilities. There was a shared bathroom and a large communal kitchen. It was not as good as Brunswick Gardens but was only intended as short term accommodation until she had worked out the next plan of action. And she found work at the Fifth Avenue Boutique on the King's Road, just two stops away on the tube.

Relief. Freedom. No John. No Sheena. No-one to question her or care; no-one for her to be involved with in return. Yes, a relief for a while – and then the loneliness crept in.

Katy. She'd phone Katy.

"Oh I wish you'd phoned earlier, Emma. I would love to come down and see you but I'm just about to start my final year and it's panic stations! But how are you?"

"Oh great," lied Emma, bitterly disappointed, tears filling her eyes. "I've just moved into a new pad – it's really groovy. And I've moved on from Miss Selfridge to Fifth Avenue on the King's Road."

"Wow Emma! King's Road! You really are in the heart of things! What's it like? All those fabulous boutiques!"

"Yeah, it's really cool. If you came down we could shop there, I'd show you where it's all happening, take you to Speakers' Corner in Hyde Park." But Emma's enthusiasm was thin and Katy sensed this.

"Oh Emma, honestly I'd love to, but I really can't. Hey, it's only three months to Christmas; maybe you can come back home for a while?" Katy hesitated a moment before asking cautiously, "Are you still in touch with John?"

"Uh huh, he came down for a bit in the summer when I was in my last place, but it kind of didn't work."

"Did he? I didn't know that. Still, I guess it must have been weird not having seen him for so long. Maybe at Christmas it'll be easier, back here in Newcastle on your old home ground. It would be really sweet if you could get together again, you know."

"No, I don't think so." Emma twisted her hair nervously around her fingers, the scene of their last row flashed through her mind. "He does my head in these days." She wanted to tell Katy more, but couldn't think what to say. It was too melodramatic and confusing to elaborate on. "But I really want to see you, Katy. I just wish I didn't have to go home if I come back for Christmas."

"Why ever not? I bet your mum and dad are longing to see you – it's been nearly a year since you saw them."

"I don't know. Bad feeling, bad vibes, I guess." Emma paused. Her head hurt, her heart hurt. She wanted Katy to make her feel better, but she didn't know what was wrong. "Katy..."

"What?"

"I'm not good. I'm not well."

"God, you're not pregnant are you?"

"No, of course not. I'm just kind of down about things."

"Oh Emma, look – why don't you come back now? It would do you the world of good, we can have a real long talk like old times –"

Tears trickled down Emma's cheeks. She couldn't speak.

"Are you still there, Emma?"

"Yes."

"Will you do that? Just come back – if only for the weekend?"

"I can't... I couldn't. I couldn't bear Mum and Dad, the house, my bedroom."

"Why?"

"I don't know. I don't know anything. My head's all bad. It's like I'm crazy." Suddenly Emma felt sick. Her stomach heaved. "Listen, I'll try. Thanks Katy, I've got to go – someone's banging on the door."

"Oh Emma – "

Emma opened the door and walked out into the deserted street.

The watery, autumnal sun shone, its reflection sparkling on The Serpentine. Although October, it was warm enough for Emma to take off her shoes, carrying them in her hands, and walk through Hyde Park barefooted. For once she was having a happy day. She kicked the leaves with her naked toes, smiling contentedly as she watched children playing, couples embracing, families with dogs.

She didn't see him at first.

"Season of mists and mellow fruitfulness,

Close bosom friend to the maturing sun…" she mused to herself, inspired by the russet crunch of leaves underfoot.

Then she saw him, out the corner of her eye. A dark, slim young man – faded denims, open cheesecloth shirt, Indian embroidered waistcoat, long deep brown hair and droopy moustache – and he was looking at her. Wow! She returned the gaze briefly before continuing her solitary walk self-consciously; her head tossed back a little now, her step somehow flirtatious. He walked to an ice-cream van parked next to the water's edge and bought two giant ice-cream cornets complete with chocolate flakes.

Emma took hers and laughed. They walked together, licking their ices. He was outstandingly attractive and she felt way out of her depth, not realizing that he felt exactly the same way. After a while, he gestured for her to sit next to him on the grass.

"I'm Nicholas." His brown eyes danced behind a cultured, deep, well educated voice.

"I'm Emma." Was that cool enough? Boring? Too cool? The image was working overtime. She scooped her hair back over her shoulder and offered a smouldering, teasing smile.

Nicholas was a follower of the Mahareshi Mahesh Yogi, holy man from India – now gathering increased acclaim since the Beatles declared devout interest in his teachings. He had recently returned from San Francisco where he discovered his most important quest in life was to search for "Truth" in meditation – often with a little mind-bending help from acid trips. He called himself a real new age hippie, advocating free love alongside spiritual peace and harmony. Financially, he survived on a generous parental allowance and lived rather splendidly in a flat off Marble Arch. Emma was mesmerized.

Nicholas plucked a long blade of grass from the ground, his eyes riveted to Emma's; he sucked the stem before placing it between her lips. "You're beautiful," he murmured.

Emma returned his stare shyly, the blade of grass resting softly in her mouth.

"I mean it," he insisted.

Slowly Emma withdrew the grass from her lips and blushed.

"Thank you," she said, a little unsure of what to say.

Nicholas lay down on his back, staring at the sky. His Levis were faded almost white over his knees. "I know this may sound surrealistic, but I feel I know you. Maybe our souls have connected before? Have you ever tripped on LSD?"

"Er, no…I've smoked pot."

"It really heightens perception. I believe we need to listen to the subconcious, open ourselves and find harmony with one another."

Emma felt naive. She kept silent while he continued. He propped himself up on one elbow, flicking his long hair over his shoulder. "Will you come with me…?" Emma wasn't quite sure what he meant. Nicholas then stood up and gently pulled her to her feet. "Come home with me. I live near here."

Mesmerized and completely caught up in the romance, she allowed herself to be led to his flat on a small cobbled back street tucked privately behind the hustle and bustle. The flat was luxurious; he lived with two homosexual men, and a young actress waiting for her big break. Nicholas briefly introduced them to Emma, they nodded and smiled as he carried on to the bedroom. His own huge bedroom. Once there, he closed the door behind them, and slowly moved towards Emma and undid her blouse.

"You are so lovely." And he led her gently to the bed.

Emma felt nothing, well, not sexually anyway. She was shocked at her own daring. So now she was a candidate for free love. And a hippie. Yes, a hippie.

"I want you to live with me," said Nicholas.

Emma lay on her side, Nicholas next to her – their bodies close but no longer touching. His smell was alien, his shape unfamiliar. She thought of John. He had been her only lover until now. Her body responded to John's, but nothing had happened at all with Nicholas; in truth, she'd been slightly repulsed if anything even though he was good looking. Yet here he was asking her to live with him.

She considered the proposition in a practical, cool-headed way.

"I would like that," she heard herself saying.

Nicholas kissed her on the forehead, got up and pulled on his pants. "Good."

It was all so unreal and dream-like, so out of touch with common sense. She glanced around the room. In the middle stood a large oak table with books and papers stacked high, underneath lay more books – on religion, Buddhism, astrology. There was a chair brimming with a pile of fashionable clothes, an expensive record player stood on the floor next to a scattered pile of records. The Mahareshi Yogi smiled down at her from a huge poster on the wall, underneath it said "The Love of the Guru".

Ten days later Emma moved in. She shared Nicholas's room and quickly felt an integral part of the household. They were a strange, offbeat group, heavily into drugs and each carrying their own psychotic luggage. Nicholas showered Emma with love and adoration but it was false, part of a game – which at least made it safe for Emma who wanted intimacy without intimacy. Then there was George, twenty-seven, a homosexual on eight mandrax a day (he boasted) and the lover of Dominic – nineteen, effeminate, always clutching a soft pink cushion like a small child hugging his teddybear. Janet, the actress, floated between them all chanting divine messages from Socrates and the Tibetan Book of the Dead.

Strangely, Emma felt quite safe, ensconced in a pretentious, non-judgmental love, enjoying a satisfactory sense of security with companionship and privacy. No-one asked personal questions – nor would a mind-blowing outburst demand explanation. It was very liberating. Just one thing unnerved her: when Nicholas spoke of Dominic's hang up.

"He's fucked up because he's adopted," explained Nicholas. "Reckons he can't go forward without a past, that he has no identity. No roots."

Emma cringed, but remained detached enough to ask more. After all, Nicholas knew nothing of her own past so she could probe openly without exposing herself.

"Surely he has good adoptive parents?"

"He says he's never been able to relate to them. Everything was okay until he was a teenager, then he says he got freaked out because he didn't know who he was."

"Oh that's awful. Can't he find out more about his past? At least learn more of his background?"

"No. Closed shop. His adoptive parents refuse to talk about it, say they don't know anything."

"Why would they be like that? Surely they want to help him?"

"Apparently not. They just told him his biological mother didn't want him; that his loyalty should be with them, the parents that brought him up; that they've given him a good life. But he still feels abandoned."

Emma was disturbed. "Should it matter that much? I mean, well, he's had good parents. Don't you think its just Dominic being paranoid?"

"Don't know." The subject obviously wasn't of much interest to Nicholas but Emma persisted.

"Anyway, he doesn't live at home now. He's nineteen, can't he find his birth mum for himself?"

"He's been told she never wanted him so what's the point?"

"I bet she did."

"Anyway, he hates her."

Mrs Hargreaves opened the letter.

Emma had written giving her parents her new address and asked if it might be okay to come home for a couple of weeks at Christmas. Emma's mother felt so distant from her daughter now and memories of that once sunny, laughing little girl were like a figment of her imagination. But she had written back to her saying how happy they would be to have her home.

Her husband had mellowed during the last year since Emma had gone. For herself, she missed the old happy days with Emma – those days before she'd met John and got herself into trouble. It seemed Emma had had no reaction whatsoever to the adoption – it had been as if she'd never been pregnant. No sooner had the baby been born than she was off out with John again, parties and socializing. And now there she was enjoying this trendy wild living in London; not that Kathleen approved of that kind of life, but she was at least pleased Emma had suffered no repercussions, no sense of loss.

She herself had never spoken to Jack about the baby – never told him how she'd pined for her grandson. Nor would she ever tell where the child had gone. She had found that out. The social worker had carelessly let a couple of snippets of information slip… She would take the secret to the grave with her.

Dominic and George sat crosslegged side by side, arms around each other, the pink cushion resting on Dominic's lap. Janet squatted next to them, her favourite meditating position. Nicholas and Emma completed the circle. Frankincense oil perfumed the darkened room, mingling with the smell of cannabis. A grey haze of smoke lingered over their heads.

"Oooommmm," hummed George, eyes closed.

"Oooommmm," they all joined in emitting a long, continuous droning sound – from the base of the stomach, or soul, as Dominic said. Emma's mind was linked with the others; sheer escapism in drugs and droning. Her eyes closed, her thoughts emptied, her consciousness drifted. She'd survived her first LSD trip three days previously; Nicholas promised to be with her on her virgin cocaine journey – but that would be after Christmas. Right now, Emma felt sky high on pot and their communal resonating hum.

She didn't think or even know it was November 24th.

Somewhere in the world, a little boy was having his first birthday.

Chapter Seven

"Yeah, well I might be going with Nicholas to India, that's where it's all happening. He's a follower of the Mahareshi Yogi." Emma touched the beads round her neck before lighting another cigarette. "I tell you, the guy is so…Katy, he really knows what it's all about."

Katy felt she hadn't quite grasped what Emma was telling her. It didn't sound like Emma speaking. "Oh that's great," she offered politely. "Are you in love with this Nicholas, then?"

"Mmm, that's a limiting question." Emma drew hard on her cigarette. "Kind of. It's more a soul link – above the realms of physical pleasure and more into a spiritual understanding of the truth."

"You mean the sex is crap?" risked Katy, grinning.

"Katy, you just don't understand. It's transcendental. Love-making is an expression of harmonizing – it doesn't have to be mind blowing."

"Not like John then?"

"Oh forget it. You are on basic ground level. John was primary stuff. I'm more enlightened now. The past is history. London has expanded my awareness." Emma scanned her eyes around the coffee shop scornfully and drank the remains of her coffee.

It was only four pm and already dark. The coffee shop offered warmth from the cold, January air outside, but Katy felt a distinct chill in Emma's attitude towards her. She tried again. "When I spoke to you on the phone a few months ago, you said you were down about things, that your head felt bad. How's things now?"

Emma drummed her fingers on the table and looked agitated. "Oh that was just John. And the pad I was living in. Nah, I'm great now. Finding Nicholas has really got me sorted out. He is so mature, and the group of us get really smashed out of our minds every now and then, like it's really great to blitz your head and get it together."

Katy looked at the yellow nicotine stain on Emma's fingers. "What about John? You know, when he came to stay with you?"

"Oh he is such a conceited arrogant Northerner. I just told him to piss off in the end."

"I saw him last week with his new girlfriend. She's really pretty."

For a moment, Emma felt jealous.

She wanted a joint. To be with her own people. Katy was so ordinary. "So how's college then?" sighed Emma blandly, changing the subject.

"Well, now Christmas is over it'll be all work towards the final assessment in June. Then I don't know. Maybe work through the summer and then travel for a bit. Do you think you'll stay in London?"

"I don't know. Like I'm with Nicholas, but we aren't like – bonded or anything. I may go to India – or even America. The inspiration will present itself when the time is right."

Katy couldn't take any more. This wasn't Emma. This was a fake. She seemed obsessed with drugs. Katy knew her old friend could be in serious trouble if she wasn't careful – yet she couldn't reach her through this hard, brittle exterior. What had made her change so much from someone so sweet, happy, sensitive and honest?

"Listen Emma," Katy looked at her watch apologetically, "I've just remembered I've something to do. I really must go. Maybe we can have another coffee before you go back, but whatever, keep in touch, won't you? And–er, if you need me, for anything, let me know. Okay?"

"Oh, yeah. Okay. Sure thing." Emma gaped, somewhat surprised.

"And give my love to your parents."

"Yeah, sure…"

And she was gone. Emma left shortly afterwards. She couldn't talk to anyone in Newcastle anymore. She thought about her friends in London and they didn't seem real either. It sometimes felt she didn't belong anywhere, that she couldn't feel any sense of self.

Almost as if she was dead inside.

As she approached the bus stop, a tap on the shoulder brought her back to earth.

"Emma, isn't it?" The face seemed familiar, a woman about her mother's age with a pushchair. The woman stooped down momentarily to wipe the child's face. "Mrs MacKenzie. Jane's mum," she smiled.

"Oh! Oh, wow...is this? " she nodded towards the small boy, "is this–?"

"Yes." Mrs MacKenzie beamed, her face bursting with pride. "A wee canny rascal, I can tell you. Do you know, he's fourteen months old now and toddles about all over the place!"

"How is Jane?"

"Back at college. Doing very well now. And how are you, Emma?"

"Oh, fine thanks. Fine. In London...you know."

The baby started to whimper.

"Well, I must be going, Emma. Lovely to see you – hope everything goes well for you." She gave Emma a maternal, knowing smile. "Give my regards to your mother and father."

"Yes, I will do, thanks. Give Jane my best wishes. Bye..."

It didn't seem fair. Emma felt cheated. She fought the intrusive vision of her own son – nearly fourteen months and, no doubt, toddling. Her head swam. Depression, loneliness and fear washed over her. She felt sick. She thought these feelings had gone. What was the matter? This was a bloody shit day.

"I'm sorry, Emma." George put a comforting arm around her shoulder. Dominic watched the scene from the other side of the room, clutching the cushion to his chest. "I only got back myself a couple of days ago and he'd gone by then – just this note."

Emma read the note again. It wasn't even addressed to her, but "The Commune" – as he called it.

I love you all – but Mahareshi calls. Enlightenment is now another journey for me. Gone to Rishikesh to pray above the Ganges. I leave you with my thoughts of peace and harmony – Happy New Year, Nicholas XXXX

"What do I do now?"

"Stay as one of us. You know we love you."

"But Nicholas has been paying the rent – I can't possibly afford to stay here and pay that sort of money."

"What do you want to do?"

"I don't know. Have you got any gear? Dominic, have you got any acid?" Emma kept running her hands nervously through her hair.

"Not LSD, man; that last trip freaked me out." Dominic was sitting down, hugging the cushion tightly to him. "I thought my head was breaking up, man. I tell you, a bad time is not worth the hassle, like mega paranoia or what."

"Sure thing. I've got some mandies, Emma."

"Oh fab. Thanks. I need something."

The next day Emma felt awful. She'd mixed mandrax with cannabis and cider. Time to move on again. She would go and find Maxine and Clive at the Flea Market - see if they had any ideas for a job.

"Oh wow, Emma! Say, this is cool! It's really good to see you, man." Clive's hair had grown half way down his back. Beautiful. Black, shining, straight, with a middle parting. Emma had never noticed before how good looking he was. "So – how's your life?"

"Ready to change direction again, I think." Emma shrugged.

"Yeah?"

"Uh huh. You know where I am is so spaced out – like I was with this guy, right, and I thought there was something between us – but he's freaked off to India. Now there's just these two queers and a really strange girl trying to get into films. It was okay when I was with Nicholas – but it's all kind of fallen apart now."

Clive stroked his long moustache and Jesus beard, his dark eyes full of genuine concern. Apart from the occasional joint, he didn't touch drugs. He was a brown rice and lentils vegetarian. In his opinion, Emma seemed mentally unbalanced. He was about to take on his counselling role when Maxine joined them.

"Oh, wow! Emma! This is so fab!" Maxine gave Emma a huge hug. "Come and have some camomile tea!" Maxine went behind their market stall and poured the herbal drink from a flask into a paper cup. "You first," she offered.

"…anyway, so that's where I am," finished Emma, having related her story yet again to Maxine in even more detail.

"Seems your need to link with emotional cripples is because you're one, too? A common bond – as in homeopathy; like with like?" offered Clive, keen to exercise some analytical opinion.

"What do you mean?" Emma felt she didn't need analysing.

"Just that you've been living with misfits."

"They're not misfits!" protested Emma. "Nicholas has got his head more sorted than most of us – he is really tuned in."

Clive laughed.

"Take no notice, Emma." Maxine put an arm round Emma's shoulder. "I think what Clive means is, well, maybe it's a bit over the top – and perhaps you've caught some of their thinking, and you know, drugs are not such a good idea – not mandrax and acid." She too thought Emma seemed very unstable and depressed.

Emma felt her protective barrier harden. What did they know?

"How's Sheena?" Emma changed the subject. She was getting good at that.

"She's great. In the same place, living with Sandy – do you remember her, Mary Quant cosmetics?"

"Yes, I think so." Emma wanted to go now. She was feeling uncomfortable. Under scrutiny. She wanted to get away from all this. Move on. This had been a bad idea, coming to see Maxine and Clive. "Anyway, must dash. Give her my love when you see her."

"Will do. Lovely to see you again, Emma. Call by any time. Oh, in case you're interested, BIBA are looking for assistants…"

"Yeah, thanks. See you."

Emma walked away. It seemed she could only cope with solitude. What was the matter with everyone? She walked through the market stalls. Something in the air caught at her senses, momentarily paralysing her. It was cold in the market building. Someone had a paraffin heater to warm up their corner. It made her feel strangely depressed and lost about everything, but she couldn't work out why.

The BIBA boutique on Kensington High Street was not far from the market. Emma walked inside as she had done many times before. The small, cluttered store was like an Aladdin's cave with dimly lit alcoves, nooks and crannies. Diffused lighting illuminated racks of the latest clothes, a cornucopia of fashion and accessories. Soft music played unobtrusively. Emma approached a young assistant.

"Could I speak to the manageress please?"

"Sure, follow me." The assistant led Emma to another girl, little older than herself. "Isabel, this lady wants to speak to you."

The young manageress smiled as Emma explained she was looking for work. After eyeing her up and down, and asking a few general questions, Isabel offered Emma a job.

This time it wasn't a bedsit. Enquiries at an accommodation agency produced a 'third girl to share' offer on Earls Court Road. A brief visit to the flat and meeting one of the girls proved it to be adequate.

Back to Nicholas's, bag up her meagre belongings and try to manage the move in one journey.

She alighted the tube at Marble Arch, reflecting wistfully that her days of living the life of the idle rich were over. Nicholas had never told her much about his background, but she understood from George that he was the son of an extremely wealthy, eminent politician. It was back to nine to five and beans on toast.

She turned into their street and instantly recoiled in shock. An ambulance and two police cars surrounded the flat. In the obvious commotion Emma thought the place had been busted for drugs and almost turned on her heels, then she caught sight of what looked like George crying. Janet stood at the open front door, two ambulance men wheeled out a stretcher. Dominic? It looked like Dominic...

Janet noticed Emma and raised her arm. "Oh Emma, it's awful. Dominic – he's, he's..." Janet just held her hand to her mouth. She looked white.

Emma was with them now. A police officer approached. "Do you know these people?" he asked. Emma heard George make a loud, gulping crying sound. What the hell was going on?

"Er, yes... I live here." Should she have admitted that?

Janet drew close to Emma, ignoring the policeman. "He's overdosed. Dominic's overdosed."

Emma felt sick.

In a blur of events, the ambulance drove off with George accompanying his boyfriend. The police came into the flat and took some details – they left shortly with the assurance they would be in touch again soon. Amazingly they didn't investigate the property and Janet and Emma whizzed around for a couple of hours after they'd gone disposing of any evidence of drugs. Emma never said a word about her new flat. It suddenly seemed wise to exercise discretion.

George returned. "He's dead," was all he said.

There followed what Emma considered to be her "quiet period". The two girls in the Earls Court Road flat were not friends by choice. Sally worked in the accounts department of a shoe shop in New Bond Street and Margaret worked as a secretarial 'temp'. They were wholesome girls, not into drugs or alcohol and both hoped eventually to fall in love, get engaged and marry some professional, decent young man. Just what my mother wanted me to be like, thought Emma.

This suited her. She decided the two flatmates were intimidated by her, they seemed reluctant to make the barest conversation. In truth, they considered Emma to be strange and affected and wished now they'd never invited her to join them. Their ignoring her was a ploy to get her to move, but it served merely to keep her contentedly aloof. She was working quite happily at BIBA's and enjoying closer friendship with the other girls there – especially with Joanna. She never went near the old flat and George and Janet never knew where she had gone.

Most nights Emma now stayed in alone, spending hours in her bedroom playing records, experimenting with makeup and wondering what to do next. She wasn't happy or unhappy.

Joanna and Emma were window shopping down the King's Road one warm Saturday in May. The King's Road bustled with young people and there was an almost carnival atmosphere with a slow but steady stream of trendy traffic weaving up and down the road.

So when a flower power psychedelic painted mini van hooted at Emma and Joanna, they took no notice.

A little further on, the same vehicle hooted again, now with windows wound down and the sound of a male voice shouting "EMMA!!"

Emma stopped in her tracks. "Oh wow, Nicholas!" she exclaimed, genuinely excited to see him, "You're back! How was India?"

"Hey – just scramble in the back – the pair of you! We're off to Anthony's…" Nicholas, who was the front passenger nodded to his young, attractive male driver. "Only down the road – coming?"

Emma threw Joanna an inquiring look. She nodded, clearly happy with the day's new injection of fun, and indecently exposing lots of leg and knickers, the two girls clambered into the back.

The mini van drew to a halt in Sloane Square.

"Oooo – posh or what!" grinned Emma.

"Yep. You're back with the jet set, kiddo," said Nicholas. Then with an apologetic smile he said quietly into her ear, "Sorry, you know, about everything."

Emma shrugged casually, as if to imply it didn't matter.

"No, honestly. It was a bastard thing to do." He tousled her hair affectionately.

Nicholas was actually living back at home with his parents since his return from India. He had at first gone back to the flat to find it occupied by strangers. His flatmates had left no word but as Nicholas felt bad about his speedy exit, he just decided to drop it and start again.

Emma told Nicholas about Dominic.

"Oh God, no. That's fucking awful," said Nicholas, visibly shaken. "What – deliberately or by accident?" Emma shrugged.

Four hours and several joints later, Nicholas invited Emma to join him on a trip to New York.

"You can't just say 'Come to New York'," laughed Emma.

"I just have. I've got a good friend in Greenwich Village in Manhattan, the son of a famous poet, his father was at Oxford with mine. He's always pestered me to stay – apparently last year there was a tremendous happening in Central Park and when the fuzz arrived, hippies pelted them with flowers!" Nicholas's enthusiasm was infectious and his ridiculous wealth made life seem like a game. And he was so beautiful; just looking at him, watching him talk with his smooth, upper class accent, was a feast in itself. What a pity she didn't actually fancy him.

"What about your friend in wotsit village? Won't he mind?" Emma visualized some sleepy, quaint corner of New York with thatched cottages and roses round the door.

"Nah, it would be cool, man. Real cool."

Emma laughed. "You bet. I'd love to come!"

Chapter Eight

Nicholas's friend, Alex, lived with his girlfriend, Anne, in an apartment on the corner of Bleeker Street in Greenwich Village, a short walk from the Hudson River. They owned a colour television. Emma had never seen a colour television before.

Alex called himself a poet-cum-philosopher but wasn't really either. He was 27, quite small, dark and rat like. Anne was also petite with long golden hair, seemingly delicate but actually quite shrewd, calculating and astute.

Emma felt very insecure. The obvious wealth was now unnerving. It was all too strange; even being back with Nicholas seemed unfamiliar and pangs of something akin to homesickness hung over her.

Also, she wasn't very well. When she went to the loo, it burnt her. Moreover, sometimes the need felt terribly urgent – but when she went, there was little more than a painful dribble. She felt too embarrassed to mention it to Nicholas and certainly not to Alex or Anne.

Nicholas was as charming as ever, pouring out his cliche-filled speech; superficially affectionate. As the nearest thing to security around, Emma found herself somewhat dependent on his presence.

One day, the four of them were smoking pot and making pretend plans for something called a Be-In which Emma couldn't follow at all, when another visit to the loo produced blood. Pale and shaken, Emma rejoined her friends. She knew now she'd have to say something.

"I'm not right," she muttered to her friends apologetically.

"How do you mean?"

"I don't know. I'm bleeding…"

"Oh God, you're not–" said Nicholas.

"No. Not there." She squirmed uncomfortably and looked at Anne.

"Don't worry," she drawled kindly, after Emma had finished, "sounds like cystitis. We'll have a word with our doctor."

Dr Bartholemew had a surgery off East 42nd Street. Emma had told them she couldn't possibly pay any medical fees, but Alex had refused to let her even think about it. The doctor was a distinguished middle aged man, with the good looks and mohair suit that money can buy. Emma explained her problem.

"Aha," he nodded, tilting back in his leather studded chair, smiling, "a typical case of mini skirt-itis I think!"

"I'm sorry?" That didn't sound quite like what Anne had said.

"Mini skirt-itis. Your short mini skirts allow the cold air to chill the bladder which results in localised inflammation. Let's just have a look at you – if you'd care to slip onto the couch."

Dr Bartholemew gently pressed her abdomen and groin, lifting her dress up to her middle. After some gentle probing, he looked at Emma over the top of his gold rimmed spectacles.

"Married?"

"I'm sorry? Oh, er no."

"Boyfriend?"

"Yes…"

"Could you be pregnant?"

"Er, no." Emma flushed uncomfortably.

"Have you ever had a baby?" Dr Bartholomew now turned away to write down some medical notes. What should she say? Should she say no? Did it matter – medically? Would he be angry with her?

"Yes," she offered quietly. It was very strange admitting to it because she denied the event so strenuously in her mind.

He looked up at her. "Where is your child?"

Emma's throat constricted, but he didn't seem angry. "Adopted."

"I'm sorry." He pulled down Emma's dress and stood in a manner that showed he'd finished examining her. "In England?"

"Yes." Emma paused. "He'll be two in November." It was weird saying this, but something in the doctor's manner was comforting, like an emotional caress.

"How do you feel about that? Has it been difficult for you?"

For God's sake let's stop this, thought Emma, his kindness would make her cry if she wasn't careful.

"I'm fine thanks. It's okay – bit difficult at the time, you know, stigma and all that. But it's all history now."

"Mmm. Mmm. Most difficult for you, I'm sure…"

Emma wondered why he seemed so understanding. Not that she would say she'd ever really found it difficult.

"I want you to take these, one tablet four times daily." He smiled at her, almost paternally. "This will reduce the inflammation quickly, but try and cover up a bit more – oh, and ease off the lovemaking for a while."

He smiled and Emma left to join her waiting companions.

"Okay?" they asked.

"Yeah, fine."

The four of them walked to 5th Avenue and passed shops that made Emma drool, then by the Rockefeller Center and Central Park by the Plaza Hotel.

She had admitted she'd had a baby to the doctor. The words echoed in her mind – "He'll be two in November". Where was he now?

"You're quiet," noted Nicholas. "Sure you're okay?"

"Yeah, sure. I'm fine."

Where was her baby now?

Nicholas sensed Emma was preoccupied with something.

"I'm taking Emma to Sheep Meadow, show her where it all happened last year."

"Cool. See you later."

Where was her baby now?

They sprawled on the grass. It was warm, early June. The area was a magnet for hippies and scattered around were groups and pairs indulging in their self-made atmosphere of peace.

"What's the matter?" he asked as they sat down.

Emma looked at him. For the first time since Oliver had gone, she felt inclined to share it and brave enough to take the risk. Maybe she would be better to talk?

"The doctor asked me something…personal. And I told him."

"Oh?"

Her heart was like a spring-loaded door. It kept closing. She went quiet.

"Do you want to tell me?"

Yes. No. Yes. No.

"Maybe."

Silence.

"I had a baby. Eighteen, nineteen months ago." There. It was out.

Nicholas stared at her, his mouth agape. "Oh wow. That's heavy, man. Where is it?" Visibly moved, he ran his hand repeatedly through his hair, shaking his head in disbelief.

"He. It's a 'he'. I don't know where he is. He was adopted."

"Oh fuck. Dominic."

"It's okay. They aren't all like Dominic I'm sure. But the doctor asked me if I'd had a kid. It's just thrown me, that's all."

"Shit. Oh wow. I'm sorry. Why didn't you say anything before?"

"Because, " for a moment Emma was confused, "...I don't know. It's bad, isn't it?"

"Why? The shame?

"Well, yes – the shame. I mean, like, I know it's the swinging sixties – but there's still a stigma attached to illegitimacy."

"Maybe to old fogies, but not me! Hey, this is heavy."

Emma looked at him, saw his deep, sad eyes and furrowed brow. And she'd told him. She'd actually told him. He cared. But where was her baby now?

"No wonder you're fucked up. No wonder you're unreachable."

"Am I? Is it? And who's unreachable? You are – not me."

"You and me, babe. That's our link. But Jesus. That's heavy, man. You're fucked up; I'm fucked up."

"Why are you – 'fucked up'?"

"My old man."

"Who is he?"

Nicholas told her and she gasped.

"But surely, you could have it made?" she asked.

"Yeah, sure thing. As his son. But I'm me – I don't want those expectations levelled at me. I need to find my own identity."

They both lay down, side by side, flat on their backs staring at the cloudless blue sky. After a few minutes, Nicholas sat up and looked hard into Emma's eyes. "How the hell have you coped with losing your baby?"

Emma winced guiltily. She had never spoken about the baby before, yet Nicholas's interest was kind, not intrusive. She hesitated.

"I mean, how old was it, I mean he, when he went?"

"Ten days."

"Do you know where he is?"

"Oh no. No. You never know that."

Nicholas ripped the cellophane off a new packet of cigarettes and offered one to Emma. She took it gratefully. He seemed loaded with curiosity but not sure where to start, what to ask. His absolute lack of inhibition enabled Emma to open up slightly.

"What about the parents? Do you know who they are?"

"No no. It's all top secret." Emma put a finger to her lips. Nicholas raised one eyebrow, disapprovingly, Emma thought.

"Who was the father?"

"Someone called John."

"Did you love him?"

"I think so, once."

"Where is he? Didn't he want the baby?"

"We were too young…"

"Did you want to give your baby up, then?"

Emma drew hard on her cigarette, held the smoke in her lungs and exhaled slowly. The dead weight emptiness she used to feel loomed near, but with it now was a dull pain, a long way off.

"It wasn't like that. There wasn't an option."

"But surely, I mean if it was us – there's no way I'd let you give it up. What on earth can that feel like?" He said the last sentence to himself quietly before resting a hand on hers. "Does it hurt now? "

Sweet Nicholas, but Emma was feeling tired now.

"No," she admitted. "The minute he went, it seemed as if a door closed in my heart."

The door closed.

"Jesus, I'm sorry. Oh wow. Have you talked to anyone about all this? Like I mean, this needs therapy, man."

Emma laughed. "No. But I didn't get kicked out of home, so that was good. My parents 'stood by me' as they say. It's okay now, really. You're giving me a hard time, Nicholas. Ease off a bit."

Nicholas tried to smile back, but remained perturbed. "Sorry. But don't you see – you're freaked out, screwed up because of this." He stroked her hair and rested a comforting arm around her shoulders. She was aware of him touching her. They had made love once since finding each other again, but had immediately slipped back into a platonic relationship. Theirs was a strange friendship based on looking good together, not physical contact. His gesture now was uncomfortably and intrusively loving.

She felt mixed up. His concern and affection unnerved her. Like the doctor. Was she psychologically disturbed? Perhaps it was more comfortable dismissing it as "one of those things", and putting it all behind her. Wasn't that the right thing to do? It was frightening. She didn't want to talk about this anymore. Not ever.

"What was his name?"

"Oliver. Look…I don't want to talk about it."

Nicholas pinched the stub of his cigarette and squeezed it back into the packet. He never littered anywhere with cigarette stubs. Said it was disgusting. She passed him the stub of her own cigarette.

"You know what you should do?" he said pensively. "Go home. Go back to Newcastle or wherever it is you come from. Go and get yourself a husband, a solicitor or accountant or something. Get married and have a family."

"Get lost!" Emma grinned, and punched him playfully.

"No, I mean it."

"Isn't that a kind of strange thing to say to your 'girlfriend'?"

"But we're fake, Emma. You're too good for me. You need a real person. Go home. Fall in love with a decent guy. Have a baby."

That night in bed, Nicholas fast asleep beside her, Emma reflected on the day. Perhaps it would be nice to fall in love, get married, share a home with a loving husband and have a baby – to keep. The dream seemed unreal, unattainable. She could go back to Newcastle, find Katy, look up old friends, put down roots and settle down. The quaint fantasy brought a smile to Emma's lips, but her eyes suddenly filled with longing. And for the first time since Oliver had gone, she allowed a very thin layer of tears to fall onto the pillow.

So she wasn't heartless.

There, that was grief. All done now.

Part Three

Part Three

Chapter Nine

Driving home the next day, after donating her mother's clothing and accessories to Oxfam, Emma was so preoccupied over the newspaper cutting safely tucked away in her bag, she completely forgot to be uneasy behind the wheel of the car.

How had her mother known of the baby's whereabouts? Had her mother ever made contact? Was Dad aware that Mum had known? Emma's mind was whizzing. This knowledge was hers alone; not to be shared. And anyway, she could never do anything about it as Michael didn't know she'd had a baby before she'd met him. Their marriage was on shaky ground as it was.

Also, it was a forbidden piece of information. Feelings of guilt merged with shock and curiosity. She drove the car down the A1 faster than usual, as if she was in a hurry. Normally, she crawled along in the inside lane, but her thoughts were rushing at break neck speed, the adrenalin coursing through her veins.

But how could she do nothing? Tomorrow morning, when the house was empty, she would phone directory enquiries just to check for any Brandons in the Newcastle area. Maybe she would glance through their own local directory, only to see the name.

Nothing more.

On her return, Emma's excitement could scarcely be contained. She barely drank any wine with her dinner, wanting to keep her senses sharp and in focus. She chattered excessively to Michael and Chloe, and laughed at the dog's playful antics.

In bed that night, Emma reached over to Michael, stroking first his shoulder, then working down. He responded hungrily, tenderly, and they made love.

"What have I done to deserve that?" he whispered afterwards.

"I just came over happy," she chirped.

Alone in the house the next morning Emma savoured the moment of privacy, dawdling over her scheming. She took the telephone directory off the table in the hall and placed it on the kitchen table. Having made herself a cup of coffee, she opened her handbag and got out the carefully hidden newspaper cutting, reading it again and again in disbelief, rolling the name Julian Brandon around her tongue, feeling it, hearing it. A flash of anger suddenly intruded as she digested the words: "Birth by Adoption".

"No! The birth was mine! Oliver's and MINE! They can't have that too!"

She calmed and put the cutting to one side and opened the directory. There were eight Brandons in Cambridge. None were likely to have any connection with Julian. He was born in Newcastle and he could be anywhere in the world now. She wondered what he might look and sound like, then imagined speaking to someone on the phone with the name Brandon. But what was she doing? She wasn't going to phone anyone.

No no. It was more a desire to tamper with the edges, anonymously explore an idea – no way did she mean to open up any more than a tiny corner of her secret. She couldn't. She mustn't.

But still…she could try one phone call. Just see what it felt like. It wouldn't be anyone remotely connected with Julian anyway. This was just an innocent game. What should she say? "Oh hello, I'm looking for an old school friend?" Bit corny. Offer to sell double glazing? Unsure as to what to say, yet possessed, Emma found herself tapping out the digits for the first Brandon.

"Hello?" A female voice answered.

"Oh hello, Mrs Brandon?"

"Yes…"

"Er, you don't know me, but I'm Janet Brown. I'm looking for a Julian Brandon. I've lost his phone number and am just working through the directory. I wonder if you can help me?"

"No, my dear. I'm very sorry but that name means absolutely nothing to me."

"Oh, sorry to have bothered you. Thanks. Bye."

"Good bye."

Emma replaced the receiver and realized she was wet with perspiration. Wiping her damp hands on her jeans, she could hear the noise of her own heart racing furiously. Her face was burning with exhilaration and she wobbled nervously towards the kitchen chair. She looked at her shaking hands. But it worked! She'd spoken to a Mrs Brandon – the same surname! It was quite safe. She had to try one more...

A second call was unanswered, a third unobtainable. One was an elderly gentleman extremely hard of hearing who just kept repeating "Who? Who?"

Having exhausted the list, save for one unanswered call to make another time, Emma phoned 192 for directory enquiries.

"Hello, name?"

"Brandon."

"Address?"

"I only have the town, Newcastle, I'm afraid."

"Sorry, but we need the address, Caller. Do you have an initial?"

"J or C."

"I'm sorry, I have nothing here under that initial but try again if you can get a full address."

"Okay. Thanks." Well, that was short and sweet.

Emma replaced the receiver only to almost leap out of her skin when it immediately started ringing.

"Who on earth have you been on the phone to?" demanded Michael. "I've been trying to get through for over twenty minutes!"

"Sorry, er I've been talking to Dad."

"You must have had an unusual amount to say. Is he okay? Anyway, I was calling to say George and Margaret have invited us over for dinner tonight, so there'll be no need to cook us a meal."

"Oh, right. That's good. Okay, I'll see you later then. I'm working this afternoon at the vets until six, remember."

"No problem. I might just be back first, but they're not expecting us until eight. See you later anyway, bye."

"Bye."

Emma felt bad. No more phone calls. That would have to do.

"And what about Chloe, Emma? What does she want to do?"

No response. Emma thoughts were elsewhere.

"Emma?" Michael sounded annoyed. "Margaret's asked you a question."

"Oh sorry. I was miles away. What did you say?"

"I asked you what Chloe was going to do after college." Margaret seemed rather put out.

"Well, she's written off to Leamington Spa for all their information on guide dog training and after Christmas she'll start applying for university too – she doesn't really know what to do." Emma thought she might have time to go to the central library by the Corn Exchange in the morning and just browse through the directories they had there for the north of England.

"Does it worry you? I mean, which would you prefer her to do?"

"No, no. It doesn't worry me. I'm sure she'll choose whatever feels right at the time." What towns surrounded Newcastle? There was Gateshead, wasn't there?

"Emma!" reprimanded Michael again. "Hello, anybody there?"

"Sorry?"

"Do you want coffee."

"Oh I'm sorry. My mind must be on Mum." Perhaps it should be her mother who preoccupied her thoughts. She must join in the conversation.

"When do you go to New York, George?" asked Emma politely.

George brought four coffees on a tray. "24th November. I'm looking forward to getting a bit of Christmas shopping done while I'm there; Margaret has already given me a list as long as my arm!"

24th November. Oliver's birthday.

Something was happening to Emma. Everything had been on hold for nearly twenty-nine years, surely it was too late to get churned up now? Why start thinking about him now? Maybe it was all to do with her mum dying; maybe Emma was actually grieving for her. And the newspaper cutting.

"Emma," said Michael, "you know you really aren't with it tonight. Perhaps you aren't feeling very well? George asked you if there was anything in particular you wanted from Manhattan."

"Did you? Oh I'm most dreadfully sorry. How kind of you. Mmm, well maybe a flower from Central Park?" Out the corner of her eye she noticed Michael frowning at her.

Finding a table in the reference section of the library, Emma sat herself down with the directories for Tyneside, Carlisle and Middlesborough. She had bought herself a notebook specifically for the task and painstakingly began to write down all of the Brandon's listed in the directory for each area, with initial, address and telephone number. It was time consuming and there was no time to finish. She had to get to work.

She had moved her self-imposed restrictions slightly by permitting herself to phone anonymously from telephone booths if she felt like it. She might not, of course. But what harm could come of making a few innocent enquiries? And in the highly unimaginable event of being hot on his trail, she would leave it immediately. No one would ever know.

She kept the original newspaper cutting in a pocket she had made at the back of the notebook; the notebook was placed inconspicuously in a plain brown envelope, which she then tucked into a discreet zipped compartment of her handbag.

Emma knew her preoccupation had become an obsession. She was driven by a euphoric instinct. But she didn't consciously connect what she was doing with the reality of ever finding him.

"Mr Parker wants us to choose our main sociology assignment for the exam." Chloe cut a small triangle from her lentil burger and popped it in her mouth.

"Oh?" Emma looked at her daughter affectionately. She was a pretty girl, and would be even more so left to nature. Her natural carrot hair was dyed to a dark reddened plum, short on top, with layers feathered in a scatty ragamuffin style onto her cheeks. She wore a plum coloured stone in her small nose, three rings in her ears, but no make-up. A Nirvana t-shirt hung loosely over her torn jeans.

"Mmm. Not sure which topic to go for."

"They give you a free choice these days, do they?" asked Michael.

"Well, not really. You can't choose any old thing. We've got a list."

Emma lay her knife and fork down, her appetite poor. "So what's on your list?"

"There's a few…let me just get it." She moved away from the table and rummaged in her rucksack, leaving unwanted items on the floor for Sam to sniff. "Here we are: Drugs and Alcohol Abuse…"

Michael raised one eyebrow and focused on his wife. Emma felt his gaze burning but fixed her attention on Chloe.

"…then there's Declining Family Values; The Dysfunctional Marriage; Teenage Aggression; Anorexia; Fear and Anxiety; and Adoption."

"Well, I'm sure your mother can help you out with a few of those," said Michael cuttingly. He sat upright in his chair as if to command authority and laughed, "We only need adoption for a full house!"

Emma's throat tightened. She reached for her wine and clumsily knocked it over. She stood up to get a cloth, her legs felt like jelly, and she had to steady herself holding onto the table.

"Are you all right, Mum? You've gone as white as a sheet."

"No, no. I'm fine, love."

Michael watched her shakily peel off sheets of kitchen roll to mop up the wine. Maybe the "Dysfunctional Marriage" option had struck too close for comfort.

"So what do you think you'll choose then?" asked Emma, patting the wet stain on the table, trying desperately to appear calm.

"Actually," Chloe hesitated and looked up at her mum, "I had wondered, I mean say if you don't want to, but I had wondered if you could help me with a bit about yourself on something personal. There is an area we could look at."

Emma wondered if she had a placard around her neck that stated that she had had a baby before marrying Michael, that the baby was adopted and that she was now obsessed with finding him.

"You know," continued Chloe tenderly, "on fear and anxiety, migraine, stress, driving, travel and all that."

Emma was so relieved she laughed. "Oh you have made me out to be a head case! I'm not that bad, am I?"

Chloe and Michael simply looked at each other.

On Monday afternoon, Emma succeeded in getting a reply from the last Cambridge 'Brandon' entry, previously unanswered. However, no link, so she moved on to the first page in her notebook headed "NEWCASTLE", and dialled the first number. This was more like the start of serious searching.

At some point in her continuing internal reasoning, Emma had acknowledged to herself that she couldn't stop. She had moved the finishing line yet again. Now the aim was to find him, or at least find he was alive, then leave it at that. At no point would she ever reveal who she was. No-one would ever know. Not Julian, not Michael, not Simon or Chloe. The challenge brought a courage, strength and energy she hadn't felt since being a teenager. But she was no longer racing with anticipation, realizing it was going to be a lengthy procedure with maybe no success for ages, if ever.

It was really bad again between Emma and Michael. Last night, he had approached her in bed but she'd been unwilling to respond, lifting his hand from her breasts and turning her face away. "I see. It's okay when *you* want to," he had said, pulling up the duvet and rolling abruptly to face the wall. Emma had remained silent, trapped by remorse, self-pity and guilt. It seemed she didn't care, was indifferent.

Sitting now at the kitchen table with a half-drunk cup of coffee beside her, Sam at her feet and the house empty, Emma lay her folded arms on the table and, bending forward, rested her head in them. The breakfast pots remained unwashed. What a mess she was in. What a mess she and Michael were in. And now, all this over Oliver. The future felt very fragile. If Michael ever found out about this child, Emma believed he would divorce her. So if she found Oliver, she couldn't do anything about it, could she? She might as well stop now. Before fingers got burned. Or hearts broken. Or lives shattered.

Emma still lay huddled over the table, nibbling her thumbnail. She hadn't done that for years, but the old habit was creeping back. She should stop searching. Then she could concentrate on working at her relationship with Michael. Get some new sexy underwear, black suspenders and stockings... oh, and cut down on the alcohol. Lose a bit of weight.

Yes, yes, yes. That's right.

Emma got up and filled the kettle. She gazed out of the kitchen window. The garden looked bare and wintry. Leaves had fallen off the trees and a thin, watery sun exposed a light frost sparkling on the lawn.

Standing in the booth suddenly reminded Emma of cuddling John, wrapping her arms around his young, firm body, feeling his strong jaw resting on her head, his warm breath on her hair, both of them insulated from the outside world.

What had become of John? It would be interesting to find out. Maybe, just maybe, she would do just that. Surely, he would be almost as curious as she was to learn about Oliver? It would be such a relief to tell someone. And who on earth could be more appropriate?

Emma looked at the small black shelf beside her and realized she had taken the little red notebook out of her handbag and placed it there.

MIDDLESBOROUGH

Temptation loomed. Yes no yes no. Yes. She fed twenty pence into the slot and tapped in the next "Brandon" phone number.

Half an hour and a completed list of calls later, Emma could not believe the name Julian Brandon was so unheard of. Amazingly, every call had answered; yet every one had dismissed her enquiry with "No, sorry". Surely, if he'd lived in Middlesborough, another Brandon would be related?

Emma walked out the phone box, her little red notebook clasped tightly in her damp palm. She walked on, thoughts racing but going nowhere. Seeing nothing and with no direction. She was bitterly, bitterly disappointed, so desperately sorry for herself – and strangely sorry for the young Emma of all those years ago.

What now? Still new into her search and she was already down-hearted. This was no good. Come on Emma, she reprimanded herself, don't fall down at the first few hurdles. Anyway, maybe leave it at that now. Yes. Leave it at that. And do NOT try and find John. She stopped a minute, put her little red book safely away in its zipped compartment, took out a tissue from her bag, blew her nose, wiped her eyes and walked home.

"Hello Chloe. What are you doing home so early?" Chloe was wading through a pile of neglected ironing that Emma had let mount up.

"Hiya Mum. There wasn't really anything on this afternoon so I thought I'd come back. I'm meeting Stewart at The Globe later, so I thought I'd just get a couple of tee shirts ironed."

"Here, let me take over love," Emma hung up her coat.

"It's okay Mum."

"No, you put the kettle on and make us a cup of tea. I'll carry on. I shouldn't have let it pile up like this. So how are things with you and Stewart then?"

"I really like him." Chloe perched herself precariously on the kitchen stool. "I'm helping him try to trace an old friend from his infant school in Glasgow. Apparently, he still owes him five pence."

Emma laughed. "I'm sure phone calls to Glasgow will be costing a bit more than that!"

"Well – a bit," grinned Chloe. "But not much more, and it's great fun. In fact it's escalating into an infant school reunion!"

"Oh? How are you doing that?"

"Stewart got in touch with a Glasgow newspaper and they're putting an advert in for ex-school mates from 1980 to get in touch and they'll send any replies down to Stew."

Of course. An advert in the personal column of all the northern news-papers. Why hadn't she thought of that? Clever clever Chloe.

"Oh you are a love," beamed Emma at her daughter.

By the time Michael came home, Chloe had gone out. He placed a couple of skiing holiday brochures on the sideboard but said nothing. He seemed subdued; not angry. Emma served up dinner. They ate together in silence punctuated by the smallest of small talk.

The next day Emma went to the library to continue her search. Her baby was given up for adoption twenty-nine years ago; papers were signed and the connection officially severed. Oliver's new parents would have been reassured that the birth mother would never be able to trace the child who was now their son. Wasn't she "breaking the contract"? But there again, what choice had she ever really had? She felt guilty yet she was unable to stop herself.

The *Newcastle Evening Chronicle* was her first port of call, she gave the receptionist the wording of her ad.

"Anyone answering to the name of Julian Brandon or knowing the whereabouts of this person, please contact Box no… whatever."

"Is this a missing person, Caller?"

"Well, yes and no."

"I'm afraid we can't divulge a name, it breaks confidentiality rules."

"Oh," said Emma, most put out. "In what way?"

"Sorry. Those are our rules. We cannot specifically ask for people by name unless it's through an official body."

"What about a date, or birthday?"

"Well, yes birthdays."

"Right. 'Happy Birthday November 24th. So you will be twenty-nine? Perhaps you know who I am? Please contact an old friend on Box number whatever.'"

"Do you want this to go in the next edition?"

She was getting somewhere. "Yes please, and to run every Friday for the next three weeks." That should do it, beamed Emma triumphantly.

"Thank you Caller. Let me read this back to you."

Great. Emma continued with half a dozen more newspapers covering the North, each with the same coded message and a confidential box number. Any reply would be forwarded to her as it arrived, which was a bit of a problem as far as hiding things from Mike was concerned, but he was almost always out the house before the post arrived, and she was only anticipating one letter.

One letter from her son.

From Oliver.

Just to see his handwriting, hold the paper he had written on, possess something he had touched, that was all. She could feel her heart swell with the thought. She would know he was alive. Then she could put it behind her.

After a few days, a plain brown envelope arrived from the *Middlesborough Evening Gazette* and Emma forced herself to wait until Chloe had gone before tearing it open.

This was it! She'd found him. It had worked.

What would he say? Her hands were shaking so violently that the envelope was torn clumsily apart. Her stomach heaved with anticipation. Two white envelopes were inside. Two? The handwriting on both was very poor.

"Daer Box no 6251 if you are loking for a bithday boy i might be the one you want. Twenty-five years of age and loking for a dominent friend to sort me out. Plaese call me on this number after ten pm."

Yuk! Emma opened the second one.

"Friend, I may not be the required age but I'm sure I could accommodate any particular interests on your part. I am very young at heart and am prepared to have a birthday whenever you so wish. My own personal preference is for water sport, and any party between us will be assured of more than just a cake. The 24th is fine by me. Just state the place and I'll be yours, the Birthday Boy."

Emma tearfully ripped both letters up and put them in the bin.

It was becoming so tiresome. She knew she was only a few weeks into searching but the effort had been colossal. She might as well say she'd been searching for years if she measured the obsessional hours of thought involved. And the time actually taken up phoning. Worse still, a surprising number of replies came back from the papers – all sexual, lonely or sad. Nothing from Oliver. In fact, she no longer wanted to find him through these channels. It was sordid.

She'd got round to Peterborough. Telephone booths were becoming her second home, the procedure routine.

"Hello, sorry to bother you but I'm looking for a Julian Brandon. I'm an old friend of his and I've misplaced his phone number so I'm working through the telephone directory."

"Oh dear!" laughed a cheerful female voice. "Well, you've found the right number but I'm afraid he's not here. Not even in the country right now."

She leaned against the side of the phone box to steady herself.

"Hello? Are you still there, my dear?"

"Oh oh, yes…"

Julian wasn't home right now.

Then a business-like calm swept over Emma.

"Is that Mary?" She risked.

"Well, yes. Do I know you?" She sounded so warm, open and friendly that Emma was almost tempted to tell her who she was.

"Not really, but I used to be a friend of Julian's. I wanted to get in touch with him for his birthday."

"Well, he's in Holland at the moment, but let me give you his address. I'm sure he would be pleased to hear from you."

The sense of relief. She felt as if a hole in her heart had been filled. Learning Oliver was alive stilled Emma. She had no intention of sending him a birthday card or a Christmas card. Neither Oliver nor his family need worry that their lives would be disrupted by her appearance. Emma resolved to concentrate on day to day living again, work at her relationship with Michael, make an effort to improve her state of health, cut down on alcohol and paracetamol.

Knowing Oliver was alive and knowing where he was gave her a peace of mind she felt she had never known before.

Yet underneath the euphoria lurked something; a horrible sense of foreboding. And something else, a heaviness, a bit like nausea.

Chapter Ten

"Margaret has pestered me to buy her a trial flight lesson for Christmas!" laughed George, pouring them all another glass of wine. "I buy her a silk scarf from Saks Fifth Avenue, and she wants to tootle over Cambridge in a toy plane."

Margaret pretended to punch her husband in the ribs. He laughed and grabbed her wrists playfully, threatening to move her hands lower down his body. Emma flushed; irritated and uncomfortable. Why was it easy for them yet difficult for her and Michael? Michael seemed to notice too and stiffened. Emma felt as if everything was her fault. She knew she had been in a particularly difficult mood just lately, blowing hot and cold. George and Margaret had invited them over to discuss plans for a skiing holiday.

"You'll love a flying lesson," approved Michael. "Do you remember when we had ours, George? Reckoned we were both going to take it up and buy our own plane."

"Yes," laughed George, reluctantly letting go of Margaret's hands, "only the absence of several thousand pounds stopped us. You must at least treat Emma to a trial flight to make it fair."

Emma gulped her wine too quickly and spluttered. Michael frowned at her. "Oh no, Emma wouldn't do that. She has to summon up courage for a drive to the supermarket."

Margaret and George shuffled uncomfortably. George poured Emma another wine, Michael held his hand over his glass, as though to emphasize his wife's excess.

"Are you scared of flying, Emma?" asked Margaret kindly.

"My wife," interjected Michael harshly, "is scared of anything outside her safe, predictable routine – except maybe the risk of liver damage."

Emma stared hard into her glass. She felt self-pity and anger well up within her but tightened her lips, withdrawing into herself, she heard Mary Brandon's soft, welcoming voice.

"What about skiing, Emma? You will come skiing, won't you?" Margaret's eyes focused on her.

Emma felt cornered. They were all looking at her. She downed her glass of wine and helped herself to another. Tension tightened her forehead. Was it the wine or a migraine coming on? Michael threw her a look of contempt. She valued George and Margaret's friendship but she didn't want to be analysed. Friendship without closeness, closeness without intimacy. Her glass was empty again.

"Oh, this is all too boring to talk about," snapped Emma. "Okay let's go flying, let's go skiing – there's a world out there full of heartache and deprivation, starving families, orphans abandoned, loneliness, misery. Oh yes. Let's talk about bloody skiing!"

The others stared open-mouthed. Emma resolutely filled her glass up yet again. Even Michael was too dumbstruck to stop her.

"What on earth got into you?" nagged Michael, driving home.

"I don't know," said Emma weakly. She felt embarrassed now.

"And all this bloody drinking. You've got a problem, you know!"

"Thanks for your understanding and support," the cold fresh air made her feel her dizzy intoxication. "Anyway, I don't think so."

Michael sighed resignedly, then rather unexpectedly took one hand off the steering wheel and patted her knee. "Sorry." It hadn't been long since her mother had died, and keeping an eye on Jack was an added strain. Moreover, he was suddenly frightened of the seriousness of their relationship difficulties – and he desperately wanted sex.

"I'm sorry, too," she said.

They made love that night, two separate people searching for security.

"Maybe I'll have a trial flight, too, if that's okay with you." What was she saying? But she so wanted his approval, desperately needed it, and a totally altered sense of proportion diluted her fear for the moment. This was negotiation; an effort to please him.

"You will?"

Oh dear. That's done it now.

Simon came home for Christmas and Chloe was infatuated with her brother's rather dubious stories of university life. Mmm, thought Emma privately, now she'll want to go to university and that will be expensive. But she was proud of her son, they both were – and they would be equally proud of Chloe whatever she chose to do.

Having Simon home had a strange effect on Emma, she wanted to cuddle him all the time. Any excuse and she was touching him, stroking his hair, sneaking a quick kiss – to the point that Mike suggested she lay off it a bit. Emma suspected it was something to do with Oliver, but as it just felt right she didn't question it or even try to stop herself.

In fact, Christmas was good. It had been difficult having Dad on Christmas day because he'd been depressed – his first Christmas without Mum, but everyone understood. Undoubtedly, Jack found it most important to be surrounded with his family, and they all made an effort for his benefit.

With Jack's return to Boulter Street and Simon's spring term at Brighton, Michael and Emma's detachment from each other returned. Her "trial flight" had been booked for the end of January, a respectable three weeks away. She could always cancel it on the grounds of 'flu or something just beforehand but at least Michael remained pleased with her, albeit with reservations. He found her timidity pathetic and stifling. There had been many occasions, especially on holiday, when he'd wanted to "have a go" at something: sea fishing, sailing, snorkelling, even the Big Dippers when the children were small – but it was always no, no, no. Now with Simon all but gone, and with Chloe growing increasingly independent, Michael was being left more and more with just Emma. She had always had this block, this fear of virtually everything. Even sexually she'd been inhibited, unwilling to play or experiment.

Emma came home from work one lunch time after a morning shift. She thought she was returning to an empty house, and instead found Mike sitting at the kitchen table, waiting for her.

"What's this?" Michael waved an opened envelope under her nose. His face was flushed, his jaw set.

"What's what?"

"THIS!" He thrust the envelope at her. Emma opened it, puzzled.

Dear best friend,

I hope you won't smack me for replying so late, but if you still want to see my birthday suit, maybe I can have a cuddle in it? I would like to nuzzle up to your big, soft body and then I promise to be a good boy. You can stroke me and I will please you I'm sure, for such a little boy I can give very big fun.

Please give me a ring, Jim.

For a moment Emma stared blankly, confused rather than offended that Michael had opened her personal mail. Then it registered – the adverts. Oh my God! After all these weeks! What on earth was he thinking? She almost burst out laughing.

"Well?" demanded Michael.

Think think think.

"I have no idea…" She hadn't. She had no idea what to say.

"You have no idea? This has been sent to you: Ms. Gray, Box No 6251, courtesy of the *Yorkshire Post*. I wouldn't normally open your post, but the scrawl on the envelope was indecipherable. I thought it was for me, actually – until I read it. Explain, please."

"It was a joke… er, at work. Sue wanted to find a boyfriend and we all had this silly idea only she didn't dare use her own name and address so I said she could use mine. We've all been in on it…" She noticed Mike relax but only fractionally.

Michael stood up, still looking bewildered. Shaking his head with a weak smile, he said, "That really threw me. I thought there was something going on in your life I didn't know about." He hugged her and kissed her on the cheek.

After he had gone, Emma touched the place where he had kissed her. She could smell his aftershave on her. The colour drained from her face as she collapsed onto the kitchen chair. *I thought there was something going on in your life I didn't know about.*

She had decided to write to Oliver. It was not an impulsive decision, it was pre-meditated. She wasn't able to stop herself.

On Saturday 8th February, Michael drove Emma to the Aero club for her trial flight. Margaret and George were already there.

"Are you looking forward to this?" asked Margaret tactfully.

"She'll be fine," interrupted Michael, preparing for Emma to bolt. But Emma wasn't going to bolt. She was going to be a good girl and please her husband. Anyway, a little trip in the sky was nowhere near as terrifying as her other plans.

The letter was already drafted in rough. The need to connect with Oliver was haunting her day and night. Just a short letter, that's all. Nothing more. She wouldn't necessarily expect a reply, just open a door to him.

She would have to tell Michael.

"Emma Gray?" A young flying instructor inquired. "Would you like to come with me?" Emma noticed Michael's eyes widen in amazement as she followed him.

"Hi, my name's Andy," grinned the instructor. "We're going in a single-engined aircraft called a Cessna. I'll talk through the controls with you – but don't worry. It'll all seem a bit confusing at first. Then we'll take off and climb to three thousand feet and when we're straight and level, I'll let you fly her for a while. Okay?"

Andy's light and easy banter reassured Emma, and a quite unexpected thrill washed over her. The plane seemed smaller – especially inside – than she'd imagined, but as they got in and taxied down the runway, she beamed triumphantly at George, Margaret and Michael.

"Well?" asked Michael, impressed. Emma grinned, face flushed with adrenalin.

"A natural," said Andy. "Seemed most at ease – we could have a perfectly able pilot here." Andy nodded approvingly.

Emma had guts. The realization shocked her even more than Michael. Yes. She had guts. Michael was impressed.

Now for plan B…

One morning the following week, Emma and Chloe were quietly enjoying an unhurried breakfast. Sam dozed peacefully in his basket. The windows were steamed up, it was still dark outside and a delicious smell of toast and coffee filled the spacious pine kitchen. Michael had already left for work. Chloe was munching through a bowl of muesli and Emma read the paper. She had been rather unwell the last few days and welcomed this peaceful time; Michael thought it could be delayed shock from her flight but Emma knew otherwise. Radio Two hummed softly in the background with Derek Jamieson chatting amiably between records. "And now–" he announced, "I have a very special guest with a remarkable story. Adrian was adopted as a baby and has just recently found his birth mother."

Emma froze.

"…and so, Adrian – tell me, how does it feel having met your birth mother?"

"Well Derek, it's changed my life. For the first time I have a history, an identity. I belong – I have roots like everyone else. It has made me very happy."

Emma held a strangled gasp in the back of her throat.

"Oh wow, isn't that just beautiful!" exclaimed Chloe.

Emma turned to look at Chloe. A God-given opportunity. Emma's heart pounded, her mouth dry as parchment. She sipped her coffee to moisten her voice. A strength came from nowhere.

"Chloe…" Chloe looked up and stared at Emma. Something in Mum's voice was different. "Chloe…when I was your age, I had a baby." It was out.

Chloe stared, unable to comprehend exactly what was being said. Baby? Where? What? Who? Mum's face was contorted with pain and embarrassment.

"You're joking." Chloe stood up. She looked at Emma, her face seemed old and grey. Her mum was having a hard time. "Mum, you're not joking."

Chloe rushed over to her and threw her arms tight around her. "Oh Mum! Where is she?" Chloe whispered.

"He. It's a he. He was adopted. I'm sorry..."

"I have another brother. Oh Mum, you poor thing, the poor boy. Where is he?"

"Holland."

"You KNOW?"

"Let's get the kettle on and I'll tell you. I'm afraid I'm making you late for college."

Chloe looked pale and shaken, so did Emma. "Does Dad know?"

Emma turned to look at her daughter. "No."

Chloe rushed both hands to her mouth. They looked at each other. "What are you going to do?" Chloe breathed the words through her fingers, her eyes wide with fear.

"Well, I could leave everything and then he need never know."

"No! You must tell him. I can't be the only one who knows!"

"No, no of course not. I shall tell him. But let's have a cup of coffee and a chat. I'm sorry, love. What a shock I've just given you."

Emma made them both a drink and re-joined Chloe at the table. She turned the radio off so that she could speak quietly and still be heard and, with great delicacy, told her shaken, enquiring daughter the facts about the pregnancy, the birth and the subsequent adoption.

"Mum, you must write to him and tell him who you are, he may really want to know. And you must tell Simon; it's not fair that I know and not him. And Dad, too. Today." Chloe bit her bottom lip. "No wonder you're always so screwed up," she added gently.

Perhaps she should never have said anything but it was too late now. The thought of telling Michael seemed worse than telling her mother all those years ago. And she would write to Simon – after speaking to Michael. Then the way would be clear.

After Chloe had finally left for college, Emma went upstairs to lie down. She closed her eyes, the recent scene enacting itself like a TV action replay again and again. How would she tell Michael? What would he say? The enormity of it. Like a violent act of betrayal. He would leave her. Of course he would. It was worse than an affair. The dishonesty, the underhand concealment of an entire human being's existence. She rushed to the bathroom and was violently sick.

Sam bounded ahead of them, following some scent trail. Emma's arm was linked into Michael's. The air was cold, they both had scarves and collars turned up. Michael was talking about work, some good order that was imminent, then about golf, a weekend somewhere. He was unusually content; Emma's effort at restoring their relationship was proving a positive success – up to now, that was. Emma was waiting for a gap in his incessant chatter.

Eventually, there was one.

"Mike." A hollow and endless pause followed. "You know in 1966, before we met, I had a baby."

Silence.

"Did you hear me?" she whispered.

"What do you mean?"

"I had a baby. He was adopted."

Michael took his hands out his pocket, unhooking her arm. He didn't say anything. Sam bounded back up to them and away again.

"Who's?"

"John's. I've told you about him, he's an old boyfriend."

"Why haven't you said anything about this before?"

"I… I couldn't. It didn't seem to matter, it wasn't relevant. Then it was too difficult – but now, I've kind of found him."

Michael walked away from her. He walked in a circle. He ran his hands through his hair and walked in another circle. Then he walked towards her and away again.

"Jesus fucking Christ!!" he spat into the cold air.

Anger would have been better. Interrogation easier to handle. Anything but this. Apart from Michael asking 'Who?' and 'When?' he remained unnervingly tight lipped. They returned back to the house in deathlike silence. Chloe was out. In the kitchen under the harsh glare of the fluorescent strip light, Emma was shocked to see his pale haunted face full of anguish. It scared her.

"Michael," she placed a hand on his arm. He shook it off. "Let me explain…"

He turned his back on her and went to bed. Shortly after she joined him and they lay in silence. And yet, for all her anxiety, there was a huge feeling of relief that she had told him.

The next morning, he remained silent. She made him coffee, prepared him some toast – left uneaten. As he was leaving for work, Emma swung him round and gripped his arms. "For God's sake, Michael, talk to me – I'm frightened!"

But he just stared at her, and left for work. As she heard the front door close, Emma wheeled around in frantic desperation…the door closed…in the kitchen she rushed to the kettle, turned around, rushed for a cup, ran her hands through her hair, panic…turned the tap on…the door closed…whimpered, like a child, spooned coffee in the mug…heard herself moan…the door…

"Mum."

"Oh Chloe, good morning, love." That didn't sound right.

"Mum, are you all right?"

Emma fell onto a chair and threw her head into her arms. She felt her daughter's small arm around her neck, a soft kiss on her hair.

"Oh Mum, don't cry. You've told Dad?"

Emma tried to say yes but all that came out was a choked groan.

Emma had been at work for less than an hour when a migraine forced her to return home. Michael's car was outside their house. He, too, had returned home early from work. It was 10.30am.

"Hello," she said on entering the kitchen, too emotionally exhausted to show surprise. He looked up and she noticed his eyes were red. She sat down at the table and took hold of his hands. He didn't resist and a tear rolled down his cheek. "Not good, are we?" sighed Emma softly.

She placed his hands in her lap, drawing her chair up close, and stroked his fingers as she spoke. Without any questions or comment on his part, she told him, as she had Chloe, the story of her pregnancy, the subsequent adoption, the stigma, secrecy, shame and heartache, the reasons why she had never told him, the discovery of the newspaper announcement and then the obsessional drive to find her lost son. Throughout, Michael held his head low.

Finally, he spoke. "What did you call him?"

"Oliver."

"Do Chloe and Simon know?"

"Chloe does. I'm going to write to Simon today."

"What did she say?"

"She was shocked obviously, but she's insistent I should write to Oliver and tell him who I am."

"Is she?" Michael hardened, his tears finished with. "I don't know about that."

"What do you think?" risked Emma.

"I don't know. I don't know." He stood up now, blew his nose and walked to the kitchen window, his back towards her. She watched him stiffen as he took a deep intake of breath before turning round to speak. "You shouldn't have kept something as big as this from me, Emma. Obviously, it's up to you what you do next, but…" Michael swallowed, his eyes cold and piercing, "you have put us under considerable strain. I might not be prepared to accept this."

What was he saying? Emma looked up at him, now it was her turn to protest. "But it was so hard in those days! I didn't dare tell you. I loved you too much to risk losing you, it was safer to try and forget, to pretend it never happened. Even my parents never mentioned him again after he'd gone." Emma's voice wobbled. "I never dreamt I would ever be able to find him, let alone know his name."

"Perhaps it's a shame you found that announcement. Certainly a shame you did anything about it."

"What about me? Can't you see it from my side? Or what about Oliver – doesn't he deserve to know?"

"I doubt he would want to know. I think you are playing with fire. You've caused us a serious problem, as if we weren't rocky enough. This has hit me like a bombshell and I'm not sure I can handle it. But if you take it further, I can guarantee you'll split us up - and also do serious damage to another harmless, innocent family."

Emma gaped. This was, in effect, an ultimatum. "So what you're saying is if I write to Oliver we're finished, don't write to him and we might be anyway."

"I'm going back to work. I've got an important meeting this afternoon." Emma watched him go into the hall, put on his woollen overcoat, pat the dog on the head and quietly leave.

"Hiya! You'll never guess what, Mr Parker thinks I'm heading for an 'A' with my sociology piece!" The rucksack was dumped on the table as Chloe collapsed to embrace the dog. "How are you and Dad?"

Emma shrugged her shoulders rather sadly. Chloe was so perceptive and understanding it was tempting to use her for consolation, but that would be wrong. "A bit shocked," she said.

"Have you written to Simon?"

"I've tried to, but only in rough. I've not posted anything yet."

Chloe nodded. "And Julian?"

"No, no. Not yet. Actually... " Emma hesitated, "Your dad doesn't think I ought to. He thinks it might cause even more upset."

"Who to? Us?"

"Well, yes...and to Julian's family as well."

Chloe stood up and moved over to the table, rummaging in her rucksack for books, but her mood was sober and contemplative.

"I guess Dad's cross with you for keeping it a secret. But if it was me, if I was Julian, I would want to hear from you. Even if I hated you for what you did, I would want to hear from you."

A pain, like a knife being pushed and twisted, tore inside her. Chloe sat down. She watched her mother peeling potatoes.

"Mum..." she risked tentatively, "who was the father?"

Emma stared at the peelings in the colander and paused momentarily. Slowly she turned around to face her daughter. "An old boyfriend from schooldays," said Emma softly. "His name was John."

"Where is he now?"

"I've no idea, love. I haven't seen him since the sixties," she turned back uneasily to the sink.

"Why did you give your baby away?"

Emma swallowed and looked up at the ceiling as if to tip back tears. "Oh Chloe, it was very different then. Not like it is now." Then she put the potatoes in the saucepan, dried her hands and joined Chloe at the table. "It was such a disgrace to be pregnant and not married, almost everybody shunned you. Giving the baby up for adoption was the only respectable thing to do."

"Didn't you mind?"

Emma laughed. "I was expected to be grateful. It was considered best all round. 'Minding' as you put it wasn't really an issue. I guess I must have blocked it off."

"What will you do? Now, I mean, 'cos of Dad?"

"I don't know, love," Emma sighed. "Play it by ear, I guess. See if he comes round."

Chloe nodded and a heavy silence fell over them, interrupted when Sam leapt up from his basket at the sound of a key in the door, and raced into the hall. Michael walked stiffly into the kitchen.

"Hiya Dad."

"Hi."

"Hello love," said Emma. "Meeting go okay?"

Michael ignored her, and went upstairs to the bathroom.

Simon phoned home a couple of evenings later, clearly shaken. "You should have told me sooner, Mum, that I'm not your first son."

"Well – to Dad and me, you are."

"Not quite the same though, is it?"

That night in bed, Emma lay staring up at the blackness, listening to Michael's breathing. Her thoughts went round and round. Unable to think of anyone to turn to; she didn't want to impose any more on her daughter. She felt the only true healing would be finding Oliver himself. He would understand. He would recognize her need to bond, their need… She knew it was forbidden, but anything now would be more bearable than the hostile stalemate between her and Michael. How could writing to Oliver make matters any worse?

Should she? Emma tossed over in bed. Should she write?

Blow it. What the hell. She would write. Oliver would be happy, ecstatic, emotionally hungry. After all, didn't she owe it to him? He would reply immediately. They would have a reunion and cry, laugh, smile and hug each other! Mary and Colin Brandon would be pleased for their son; Chloe and Simon overjoyed; Michael... Well, Michael would have to handle it or, as he suggested, go.

With the decision firmly settled in her mind, Emma glanced over at Michael's dark shape hunched under the covers. What did the future hold? Was she destroying them? Breaking up the family? She fell into a troubled sleep.

Chapter Eleven

It took more than two weeks for Emma to feel satisfied with the letter. Well, no, not satisfied. She never did feel it was good enough, but after two weeks she knew she would never feel happy with it.

Dear Julian,

I'm afraid this letter is going to be a shock, even though that is the last thing I want to do to you. My name is Emma Gray and I am your natural mother. Quite recently, when my mother died, I came across a newspaper cutting she had kept after your birth announcing your arrival into your adoptive parents' family. Finding this and, of course, your name, has enabled me to discover your whereabouts.

Please don't feel threatened or alarmed that I am going to suddenly appear on your doorstep. I just want you to know that should you ever wish to learn more of your biological background – I am here. I am now married (not to your birth father) with two children – Simon, twenty, and Chloe just eighteen. It has given me a great sense of comfort to know you are alive and, I hope, well; at the same time I admit to heartache and a strong need to know you are happy.

I have thought about you constantly throughout the years and offer my love and an open heart. But also, I make no demands and hold no expectations. I enclose a photograph of me and am happy to answer any questions you may have. However, I respect your privacy and wishes, and do not want to intrude into your life so I will not make further contact unless invited to do so.

Of course, I wish for nothing more than to hear from you at some time in the future.

With all my love,

Emma

Emma finally folded it, popped it in an envelope with a recent photo of herself, addressed it, sealed it, and walked with Sam to the nearest post box. Once there, she hovered – uncertain, her heart racing. Then with slow deliberation she pressed her lips softly over his name on the front of the envelope before letting it fall from her fingers into the box. As soon as she heard it drop, she gasped. "Oh my God, Sam! What have I done?"

Emma felt like an adulteress. To further compound her guilt, a postcard arrived that day from George and Margaret, skiing in Austria. Funnily enough, it had been Michael who'd finally pulled out of the joint holiday plans, though Emma (and no doubt Michael) still considered it her fault. She wondered about throwing the postcard away to avoid added aggravation but decided against it.

Emma swallowed two paracetamols with a glass of water. She had acted against her husband's wishes and as soon as he learnt what she had done, that would be it. She would have to tell him, of course. Oliv...no, Julian's reply could arrive by return of post, he might want to see her immediately, book the next flight over...and Emma wanted that so desperately. What would Chloe say? And Simon?

Emma's headache persisted. By four pm her stomach was heaving, her vision distorted and her legs had turned to jelly. A dull, crushing chest pain weighed heavily within her.

"When?" Michael lay on his back staring at the ceiling. It reminded Emma of a scene at Paul's bedsit in Heaton twenty-five years ago, when she and John would discuss the "important things in life" staring at the ceiling.

"Just a few days ago."

"What do you think will happen?" Strangely, Michael's voice sounded vulnerable, nervous.

"I don't know. I would like to meet him."

Silence.

"Why?"

"Oh Michael! Why? Because he's my son!"

"Not mine."

"No...I know that. But even raped women can love their babies. It doesn't necessarily matter about the father."

"Oh cheers."

"No, I didn't mean that. Of course it matters that you're Simon's and Chloe's father, but the fact that you aren't Oliver's – Julian's – doesn't stop me wanting to find him."

"You obviously haven't thought about my feelings."

"I care very much about you."

"Yes? Well, you know what I think about the whole thing. Why are you doing this? And it's not just us, you know."

"Are you going to leave me?"

"I don't know what to do. I don't know. You're throwing so many lives upside down. All because you stumbled on some fucking old newspaper announcement."

"I'm sorry... I can't help it."

"Of course you can help it. It never mattered before."

"It did, it did, it did! Honestly, I thought about him all the time. I just thought I would never be able to find him. That it was hopeless. That he was adopted. That that was it."

"But it never mattered enough to tell me?"

"I've told you this before. The shame attached to it. It made me feel like soiled goods. I thought if you knew, you wouldn't want me. I know I should have said – but then it was too late."

"So one day, over a quarter of a century later, you decide to tell me. While I'm trying to come to terms with that – and against everything I ask of you, you go straight ahead and write to him."

"I'm sorry. It's like an obsession. I just can't leave it, I've tried. At first I thought just knowing his name would do; then I had to know if he was alive; now I have to hear his voice...touch him..."

"You make me feel as if I'm on the scrap heap. You're giving this anonymous fantasy figure more bloody attention than you've ever given me. And how do you think Simon and Chloe are going to feel? And Julian's parents?"

Emma felt tears running down the sides of her cheeks onto the pillow. She swallowed but her voice wavered. "They'll be okay. I've spoken to his mum. She's lovely."

"Did she know who you were?"

"Well, no…"

"And what makes you think – what's his name? – Julian will want to know?" continued Michael.

"He will…" prayed Emma.

"Why? Who are you to him? He won't think of you as his mother. You're just a stranger, and an interfering one at that." Michael sighed and ran his hands through his hair. "And what about this fucking John cunt?"

"Michael, please – stop talking like this. I don't know about John. That's got nothing to do with it."

"Well, this 'kid' is going to want to know, surely?"

"So if he does, I'll tell him what I can. I'm not interested in John." Emma's voice was broken with choked tears.

"How am I supposed to believe anything you say now? I mean, what else have you kept secret from your past? Another daughter perhaps? Maybe a lover or two strewn along the way? And what about right now? Screwing some poor bastar…"

"Stop it!"

"Well what do you expect me to think?"

"Just Oliver. That's all. I got pregnant when I was seventeen and had a baby. I had the baby adopted. I paid my dues. I've never done anything else wrong in my life. Except marry you perhaps."

"Ah, I wondered when it would all start to be my fault."

"No, I'm sorry." Emma checked herself. "No, it's not your fault. I know I've done wrong. I didn't mean that about marrying you."

They lay in stony silence.

"You shouldn't have done this, Emma. The whole thing seems dangerous and totally selfish, I dread to think what the repercussions are going to be. Everything was fine before, now – on some emotional whim – you seem hell bent on messing up lives."

"Oh Michael, we weren't 'fine' before!"

"No, okay. You've always managed to make things difficult. But at least we managed. But have you thought about what kind of shock this kid is going to have? He might not even know he was adopted! Have you thought about that?"

"Yes. They promised me they'd tell him. The social services said they'd take Oliver away and give him to good, loving parents where he would be better off, and that they would tell him all about me, how much I loved him…"

A heavy silence again.

After a few minutes, he rolled away from her. "Anyway, we'd better get to sleep. It's two o'clock."

But Emma couldn't sleep. Although Michael was angry, he had at least spoken to her. The dream of meeting Julian shone as a tantalizing light in the dark. Anything was bearable in exchange for that. Mentally re-enacting the scenario again and again, she pictured their eventual reunion. He too would be aching to meet his natural mother. They would meet – where? A pub? No, too exposed. Here, at home? Maybe intimidating for Julian. Somewhere private, neutral…oh, anyway, they would meet, their eyes connecting – like she'd seen with reunions on *Surprise Surprise* with Cilla Black – they would be totally oblivious to anyone else. They would move slowly towards each other. Then she would be there, in his arms, hugging him, touching his hair, stroking his cheek – the relief, finally.

Emma rolled uncomfortably onto her side. There was this crushing weight in her chest again.

Oh please let there be a letter from Julian tomorrow.

Six weeks had gone by and no reply. What did that mean? Had he got the letter? Maybe he'd moved on before she'd sent it – or perhaps she'd got the address wrong anyway. Should she write again, via his mother? Or maybe he didn't want to know. Dominic had hated his birth mother, hadn't he?

As part of her need to re-connect with her past, Emma had also embarked on tracing her old friend, Katy. Katy Robinson, then. Emma hadn't seen her since 1969 and at that time, Katy had been planning to go to Australia.

Emma had lost almost a stone in weight and, judging by appearances, Michael was not far behind. Not that they talked about it. Nor had they discussed Oliver further. They hadn't talked about any of this since that night in bed. But at least he hadn't left her.

"I'd prefer to go to Loughborough because all my mates are going there. It has a brilliant reputation." Chloe was doing a precarious balancing act on the kitchen stool, feet hunched up to her bottom, arms around her knees.

"But Foundation Art wasn't even on your list of options a couple of weeks ago, Chloe!"

"I know. But the thing is, if I don't yet know what I want to do, like sociology or guide dog training, if I do this one year foundation course, it'll give me an insight into what I really want while getting a basic qualification in itself. Or I could just take a 'year out'."

Emma scowled. In her opinion, this "year out" business was an excuse for doing nothing. "Wouldn't you be better just working for a year – find out what you want to do that way?"

"Oh Mum, that would be so boring. I feel too young to be tied down to a work routine like that. And Stewart says…"

A clatter in the hall stopped them mid-conversation, drowned now by Sam barking.

"Post," said Chloe, sliding off the stool, "I'll get it."

She returned with three letters and, still chattering about Loughborough, passed them over to her mother. A bank statement, a telephone bill, and a handwritten envelope with a foreign stamp. Emma felt the colour drain from her face and prayed Chloe wouldn't register her reaction. She glanced briefly at the postmark. Holland. Oh my God. A reply. With casual indifference, Emma lay the mail on the sideboard and feigned renewed interest in her daughter's future plans, this time going along with anything to shut her up for the time being. She wanted Chloe to go. This was intensely private.

"We'll have a chat with your dad later. I'm sure we can sort things out." Emma's eyes kept being drawn to the sideboard. The letter was sandwiched between the other post.

"Oh thanks, Mum!"

"Anyway, haven't you got college this morning?"

"Not until this afternoon." Chloe crumpled to the floor to embrace the dog, obviously in no hurry to go anywhere.

"If I give you a ten pound note, I wonder if you might find time to buy me some vitamins from the health store. There should be some change to buy yourself a little something."

Emma held the envelope in her hands, fixated by the handwriting. The anticipation made her dizzy with hope. As she carefully unsealed the envelope, she thought how her own son – her own flesh and blood – had held this very paper, licked this very envelope. She pressed it to her lips for a moment – and a confusing wave of emotion flooded through her.

> *Dear Mrs Gray,*
>
> *Thank you for your letter.*
>
> *I must confess it came as quite a shock to me which is perhaps why it has taken me so long to reply. Naturally, I have discussed the matter with my parents and they, too, have felt quite disturbed and rather angry. They strongly believe that any communication from yourself should perhaps have been directed through professional channels as mediator.*
>
> *However, for myself, you may be reassured to know that I have indeed had a very loving and privileged upbringing; I love my family very much and enjoy a good life. I am happy to be alive which I trust is of some comfort to you.*
>
> *After some consideration, I feel it unwise to continue further contact between us but thank you for offering me the opportunity.*
>
> *My regards to you and your family,*
>
> *Yours sincerely,*
>
> *Julian Brandon*

Emma held the letter limply in her hands. She felt sick. This was, in effect, rejection. She knew she had to face everybody, just carry on, as if nothing had happened: work that afternoon, Chloe at tea time, Michael in the evening. She'd drawn a blank at finding Katy. The loneliness and sense of isolation was becoming difficult to cope with. And yet, holding the letter that he had written, seeing his handwriting and knowing he really existed, exploded her senses with love. For the first time she was feeling the pain of losing her son, and yet she didn't know whether it was from twenty-eight years ago or now.

Emma circled the room, still holding the letter. What to do? All those dreams, all her hopes and fantasies.

"Good afternoon, Adoption Department, Social Services."

"Hello, my name is Emma Gray – I'm a birth mother who's kind of found her son and lost him again. Would it be possible to talk to someone please? I'm struggling a bit."

"Oh dear, I am sorry. Just hold on a minute and I'll see if one of our counsellors can speak to you." Kindness, sweet sweet kindness. It acted like a key unlocking a door. Tears started rolling down her cheeks.

"Hello, Emma...? " Another voice.

"Yes," Emma choked, audibly distressed.

"I understand things are difficult for you right now. Would you like to come and have a chat?"

"Please," whimpered Emma and an appointment was made for the following Tuesday afternoon. As easy as that. Help was there. You only had to ask.

Michael was halfway through his dinner before he reluctantly told Emma. "Someone called Katy left a message on the answering machine."

"KATY?" squealed Emma, dashing up to replay the message. Michael watched his wife disapprovingly. Chloe concentrated hard on her lentil casserole, peeping up to satisfy uncomfortable curiosity.

"Hiya Emma, guess who! Finally got a message that you've been trying to find me – and well, here I am! Well, I won't tell you where 'here' is just yet, but my number is 010 305 293 9338 and a clue – I'm about five hours behind you! Really looking forward to a chat, it will be lovely to talk to you again after all this time. Bye for now, Katy."

"Oh wow! That is GREAT!" Emma turned now to her husband. "Katy's an old friend. I've been trying to find and thought I was getting nowhere but then I got back in touch with some others from her old college course – and I've finally struck oil!"

"That's nice," said Michael stiffly. He placed his knife and fork over his dinner, half eaten, and pushed the plate away. "Finished, Chloe?"

"Yes thanks. Can I leave the table, Dad?"

"May. Not can. 'May I leave the table.' Yes, you may."

Chloe slunk away, eager to extricate herself from whatever was going on. She was developing the art of not asking questions. An unusual trait of character for Chloe.

Emma left her dinner, hardly touched, and ran upstairs to their bedroom. Michael collected the dishes and walked over to the sink. He scraped the ample leftovers into a bowl for Sam. It was April and the nights were light until much later. Michael looked out onto the garden and noticed the lawn needed cutting. But why bother? he thought sadly.

"No answer," said Emma, coming back into the kitchen. "I'll call again later."

"So who's Katy then?" Mike put the kettle on. "Do I know her?"

"No, I guess not. It was before your time, in the sixties."

"I see." Pause. "So, she knew John, and all about…that baby?"

They both recoiled in embarrassment at his unexpected confrontation.

"Er, yes, it was all that kind of era." Emma could feel herself shoot into a shell. Because of guilt? Or self protection? She didn't know how to talk about it.

"I'm going upstairs to have a shower," he said.

"Oh Katy! It's great to find you after all this time! So how are things?" Michael had gone to bed, leaving Emma alone downstairs. It was midnight. Even Chloe was in bed.

"Great Emma, really good. Guess where I am? No you can't possibly guess. Everglades City – southwest Florida! Heard of Naples? Fort Myers? Anyway, further south and very quiet. In the heart of the Everglades, wonderful wildlife. You must come and visit me. But tell me all about your life, Emma…"

The phone conversation lasted about forty minutes and Emma cringed as she replaced the receiver, tip-toeing quietly up the stairs to bed like a naughty teenager trying to avoid trouble. She had poured her heart out about Oliver, told Katy everything. They had talked about John, neither of them knowing what had happened to him, reminisced over Newcastle, old friends, college. Oh such sweet relief! Emma was on a journey; the memories flooding back. Kate in return had off loaded her own chequered history: two divorces, no children, plenty of money and a wonderful life in Everglades City.

"That was a long phone call," said a stoney voice in the dark.

"I thought you were asleep. Yes, sorry. I'll pay." Emma fumbled in the blackness taking her clothes off.

"What did you talk about?"

She slid now between the sheets and wondered whether she should touch him, but if he threw her hand away it would be awful. He lay there, half wishing she would touch him, but if she did he would be tempted to throw her hand away.

"Oh nothing important, just chatting about what we've been doing."

"Where does she live?"

"Florida."

"Florida! Bloody hell, some phone call. Did she invite you over?"

"Well, as a matter of fact, she did." Emma held her breath. She really wanted to go.

Michael was suddenly relieved that his wife was afraid of travel. "Well you couldn't do that, could you?"

"No, of course not. I couldn't afford it even if I wanted to. Anyway, it's late. Best get to sleep." She patted his body lightly over the top of the duvet.

Michael rolled over, not quite understanding why he felt sad more than angry. What did she mean she couldn't afford it even if she wanted to? She couldn't want to; she'd never have the courage. Emma, too, rolled away from him, her thoughts busy with seeing the counsellor next Tuesday, planning a trip to Everglades City, one way or another she would have to go, and writing to Mary Brandon.

Yes. That's what she would do. Write to Julian's mother: apologize, be really friendly and non-threatening. Win her over. Emma was sure they could become really close, then she would approve and encourage Julian to meet her. Of course. And they would no doubt want to meet Chloe and Simon. Almost an extended family. It was understandable… Julian had felt inhibited to meet her. She had written straight to him excluding his parents, and perhaps that had been inconsiderate. Mary Brandon had always been the mother to comfort him when he needed it; now she would be able to share and support his – their reunion. Perhaps she and Mary would feel a special affection for one another. Yes. She must write soon and introduce herself. Emma pulled the duvet up over her shoulders and dreamed of Christmases blissfully surrounded by an ever-widening family.

Chapter Twelve

Emma posted the letter to Mary Brandon on the way to her appointment with the adoption social worker. Something in the back of her mind wondered if she shouldn't wait until afterwards, but she was sure what she had written would be received warmly.

In her letter she had apologized for causing any possible upset and went on to reassure Mrs Brandon she had no intentions of intruding into their private family life. Her communication had been purely for Julian's benefit in case he had any curiosity over his biological background. She thanked her for giving Julian a happy, privileged upbringing and hoped his existence had enriched their lives in return for the all the love and care they had given him. Emma reassured Mrs Brandon and her husband yet again that she was sorry to have caused anxiety but that they had no need to worry over her motivation or intentions. She closed with offering her love and appreciation, hoping she might have the pleasure of meeting them all one day.

Hearing the letter fall into the box, Emma walked on, quite sure she'd made some kind of amends, that Mary Brandon would be appeased and that Julian may now feel more prepared to meet his birth mother.

She entered the doors of the Adoption and Fostering Care Centre and walked up to reception. Posters adorned the walls showing pictures of happy families, all beaming and holding balloons. Other notices invited prospective foster parents to consider the rewards of bringing an older child into the family.

"Hello, I'm Emma Gray. I have an appointment."

"Oh yes," said the receptionist, all smiles and reading through an appointments diary. "Just hold on a moment, Emma." The smile tapped a number on an intercom system and then invited Emma to take a seat.

Emma felt nervous, a fraud. She wasn't there to foster or adopt. Moreover, she had never been "counselled" in her life before and had no idea what to expect.

"Emma?" A woman in her mid-thirties, generously proportioned with shoulder length dark brown hair and an open smile approached her. She was dressed loosely in comfortable clothes and carrying two cups of tea. Emma felt immediately at ease. "Would you like to come with me?"

It was very strange talking to a complete stranger about Oliver. It felt safe and anonymous. They sat in a small, private room; a large box of toys stood in the corner. Emma warmed to Amanda immediately but still found it difficult to open up: it felt like a confessional. Relating her story as an unemotional chain of events, Emma spoke of having her baby adopted in 1966, told of her mother's death and the subsequent discovery of the adoptive birth anouncement, the following search and eventual finding of Oliver. She admitted it had been a secret from her husband and children, and that it had seriously worsened her already stale relationship with Michael. Amanda winced, but nodded for her to continue. Emma told her that she'd then written to Oliver and recently had a letter in return.

"Would you like to read the letter he wrote me?" Emma fumbled in her bag and offered the dog-eared envelope.

Amanda took it. "Are you sure?"

"I would like you to." It felt a relief to unburden herself.

Amanda read it slowly then handed it back to Emma. "How do you feel about the letter?" she asked Emma.

"Hurt. Disappointed. Rejected."

Amanda nodded. "Like loss all over again?"

"I don't know about again. It feels like loss for the first time – but a double dose." Emma took one last sip of tea from the cup and placed the cup and saucer carefully on the table. She could feel tears welling up in her eyes and knew if she spoke now, she would cry. Amanda said nothing. They sat in silence. Amanda seemed comfortable with the silence, allowing the space to give Emma room if she wanted to talk; but Emma wasn't comfortable and started to fidget.

"You find this difficult?" Amanda eventually asked, gently.

Emma's chest hurt again. Tight, heavy, constricted. All that bullshit years ago about "removing her problem", that she would then be able to "go forward without the stigma of illegitimacy", that she could "put it all behind her" and "get on with life". What a bloody con! Here she was, twenty-nine years on, with a huge mass of unresolved heartache.

"All the way down the line it's been 'you naughty girl, BAD BAD BAD!'" exploded Emma, shocked now at the anger in her own voice, "All I want is… I don't know what I want." She stopped and let her head fall into her hands. "And look what I've done to Michael. Oh God. Such deceit." She was shaking. Amanda rested her hand on Emma's shoulder.

"I've written to Julian's mother now. To try and make things better. I'm such a grovelling wimp, but have I been so wrong? Have I been so bad?" Emma still had the images of that huge, authoritarian matron firmly engraved in her memory, and the two women at the bus stop who'd glared at her so disdainfully, and the disapproving ward sister at the maternity home.

"No. You're not bad. These are unfortunate labels put on you all those years ago and you need to discard them." Amanda withdrew her arm and looked kindly at Emma. " I think with finding your birth son, you're in touch with past feelings. On top of that, your letter from Julian has, to some extent, reaffirmed that disapproval from the very person you wanted on your side, and so – as you yourself say – it is rather like a double dose."

"I'd have thought all the hurt would have dribbled away through the years, or at least faded with time. It's a bit late now to suddenly find myself swamped with grief, isn't it?"

"I know, it does seem strange, doesn't it? But I'm afraid that's what happens when we block off our emotions. They don't go or fade with time – they just stay there, suppressed. They tend to find an outlet one way or another."

Emma paused uncomfortably, so involved with finding her own voice she could barely listen to Amanda. "Is what I've done illegal?"

"No," smiled Amanda, "It isn't normal for a birth mother to find information identifying her child, nor would we necessarily encourage searching without very careful consideration of all concerned. But it's not illegal.

And I'm very glad you came to see me today. I think that was a very positive move on your part and I hope you feel it can help a bit."

Amanda then shared a couple of case histories with Emma, explaining the difficulties sometimes faced by adoptive parents, their feelings of insecurity and overwhelming fear of rejection. How they, too, felt "cheated" by a system that promised they would never hear or see from the birth mother again, only to find that promise sometimes unsympathetically broken. And most of all, the anguish of the adoptee caught in the middle, already the victim of abandonment, sometimes with a deep longing to know his or her origins, yet torn with guilt at upsetting the parents. Amanda also reminded Emma that it was important to keep a balanced perspective and not become too obsessed, or there was a danger of destroying important existing relationships.

Perhaps you'd like to tell me how you and your husband are coping? He must be terribly shocked."

"We don't talk about it."

Amanda looked concerned. "Will you tell him you've seen me?"

"Good God no! We're only just coping by pretending nothing's happened."

"That must be difficult."

"Actually, it's easier not to talk."

Amanda nodded. There was a long silence. The session had come to an end. Emma felt emotionally exposed and drained. She picked up her shoulder bag and stood up, offering her hand.

"I didn't know you would support me," Emma confessed. "I thought I'd get lectured again. Thanks. If I may, I'd like to come another time."

"Let me take you to reception and we can make another appointment."

Emma stared out the car window as Michael drove the familiar route to George's and Margaret's. It was early afternoon, and the low sun offered its seasonal warmth. Wild daffodils bloomed along the roadside, backed by rolling green fields and gamboling lambs. Emma snuggled deeper into her seat, gazing out and daydreaming of hot sun, Florida, Katy, Nicholas, John and Julian. Thoughts floated around in her mind as she re-arranged fantasies from one scenario to another. Every time Michael talked, she felt he intruded into her world of make believe. She knew her thoughts were disloyal, but that did little to stop her.

"So you'll going to be okay with George and Margaret this time?"

"Of course," Emma withdrew further into her dreams.

"And not a repeat performance of last time?"

Emma shifted her gaze angrily to Michael. He was wearing his best Armani slacks and a slate blue sweat shirt, unusually casual for him, and a double dose of aftershave. No doubt for Margaret's benefit. She nearly said something but an argument now would interfere with her fantasies. She wondered why Katy hadn't had any children. What on earth did she look like now? And what about John? What ever happened to him? Next week, she would try to find John. Yes. That's what she'd do. Find John.

Michael swung the car into George's and Margaret's drive. "And don't drink too much, okay?"

Emma stuck her tongue out rebelliously and slung him a discreet "V" from her lap. He shook his head.

Margaret was wearing tight faded denims with a cream silk shirt generously unbuttoned. Her long hair was clipped effortlessly on top of her head and blonde tendrils framed her cheeks and neck. She hugged them both warmly while George put the kettle on – much to Michael's relief. Wine at 3.30pm would not have been a good idea.

On the dark, polished pine table in the middle of the kitchen lay two photograph albums – filled with photos of their skiing trip. Margaret patted them seductively. "Not yet!" she teased. But Emma was hardly bursting with anticipation. "And…" continued Margaret, "we have some rather special news, don't we George?"

George nodded towards the door. "Let's go in the living room," he said picking up a tray with four steaming mugs on it.

"Look at this one!" Margaret leaned towards Michael. Emma knew Margaret wasn't being intentionally seductive, nor could she have any idea that she and Michael were having difficulties, but when Emma noticed him press his thigh next to hers, an angry shot of jealousy ran through her. To counteract her envy, she leaned towards George, laughing too loudly at whatever he said.

"Anyway, enough of our boring holiday snaps," smiled George, "I think Margaret would like to tell you something." He smiled at his wife and raised his eyebrows as a cue.

Margaret beamed affectionately at George. "I'm going to be a grand-mother. We're going to be grandparents."

"Oh…oh, that's really wonderful," Emma struggled with the words. She felt shocked by her own reaction as much as the unexpected news. The thought of anyone's pregnancy and subsequent birth was difficult to take.

"Good for Reuben and Beth!" echoed Michael. "When's it due?"

"End of November," said George proudly, "24th, isn't it Marg?"

Why that date out of 365 days in the year?

"How wonderful," she managed politely, "And how's Beth?"

"I think we'll open that champagne," said George.

Driving back home again in the car, Michael complained angrily.

"Why can't you drink like any normal person? Why do you always get bloody drunk? You are so embarrassing. Jesus, and stumbling over that fucking rug like some inebriate piss artist."

Her head hurt. Her heart ached. She wanted to tell him how she was pining for her lost child, that she was living constantly on the edge of what seemed like a nervous breakdown; but she knew he would think her selfish, hysterical and neurotic. And maybe she was. But his attitude – rightly or wrongly – left Emma full of self-pity, and unable to talk. She snivelled all the way home, unaware of Michael's own feelings of insecurity.

"Fancy Reuben being a dad!" giggled Chloe, squeezing her sandwiches into the rucksack. Emma was clearing away the breakfast dishes and noted a long silence, unusual for Chloe.

"Mum…"

"Yes dear?"

"You could be a grandma. And not know it."

Emma stiffened. "Goodness, what a thought!"

"Did you ever write to Julian?"

"Yes. Yes, love. I did."

"And...?"

"Well, I got a letter back which thanked me for making myself available, but he didn't feel he wanted to take it further yet."

"Did you tell him about me?"

"Er, I can't remember. Yes, I think so."

"Can I write to him?"

"Oh Chloe, I don't know what to say."

"But he's my half brother. It's on my mind all the time."

"Oh my love! Is it? I'm so sorry. It all causes so much upset. Your dad's not happy about it and I think it's bothered Julian and his mother rather a lot." Emma sighed.

"Simon's not sure how he feels. But I want to know him."

"The thing is, you could end up hurt and rejected."

"I kind of feel that now. It's sad somehow. I'm confused. I wish in a way you'd never told me."

Chloe walked to the front door.

Amanda sat quietly listening.

"What's so hard," cried Emma, "is just having to carry on as if nothing was happening."

Her letter from Mary Brandon lay opened on the table.

"She's so angry and I wrote a really warm letter. Why can't she feel warm towards me? After all, I am the mother of her son. If she loves him, why not me – as his flesh and blood? It's not as if I want him back or anything. I know he's not mine. I feel really grateful to them for giving him a good, loving home. Listen to this... 'Julian is most unnerved by your advances. He is not particularly interested in your appearance and is more concerned with protecting us most fiercely. We would all rather never hear from you again.' Protecting them most fiercely! What am I supposed to be about to do?" Emma sniffed, self-pitying tears rose and mixed with her anger.

Still Amanda said nothing.

"That letter's full of the same condemning abuse I got at eighteen. I just don't need it. I don't deserve it. All that bloody disapproval again and again and again. I even feel angry with Julian in a way for keeping me out. If I could just see him, I'd be okay. Just touch him." Emma sighed, twisting a sodden tissue round her fingers. "Oh God, what I'd give to touch him. I have never yearned to touch anyone so much in my life before. What can I do to stop hurting? I feel as if I love him, yet who is he? Some strange man who I'm aching to see."

Silence.

"Perhaps," risked Amanda eventually, "it's important just to own these feelings and leave the outcome to whatever may be. This can be a help in itself even though it doesn't seem like it right now."

Emma uncurled herself and stiffened. "I think I'd like to get away from everything. Everyone. I'm sick and tired of sadness, sick and tired of me. I'm such a misery these days, I'm even getting on my own nerves."

"I wonder if it would help to speak to others in your situation?"

"Who? Birth mothers?"

"Yes. There's a group called The Natural Parents' Network, they have a monthly newsletter and contacts for support."

"Is there? I didn't know that. So there's a few of us then?"

"There are support groups for all sides of the triangle."

Emma left shortly afterwards with a collection of phone numbers from NPN, NORCAP, Adoption UK and the Post Adoption Centre. To be honest, she wondered how much counselling was helping. Yet, having said that, Emma actually felt rather more light hearted and positive, but perhaps that was because she'd decided to call into the library and borrow a book on Florida and the Everglades.

"When?" Michael shoved his dinner plate to one side, no longer hungry. Chloe kept silent.

"This summer I thought. Just for a month or so."

"A month or so! What about us?"

"Lots of couples have holidays without each other. We couldn't possibly both afford to go to Florida and you'd be bored with Katy."

"And how do you think you can afford it?"

"I'll only have to pay for the flight. Katy refuses to accept a penny for me staying with her."

Michael shook his head and ran his hands through his hair. He was confused and unnerved by the fact she had the courage to go – and alone. And yet, he was attracted to her about turn of character. And what about this kid she'd recently thrown at him? They never talked about it, and he'd shoved it to the back of his mind as though the pregnancy had been terminated. Easier to think that than to confront the idea of a son of hers they didn't know, somewhere.

Chloe got up from the table. "I might just go to The Globe for a drink."

Emma started clearing the pots from the table.

"So that's it, then, is it? You're going? You're leaving us for the summer?"

"I think a short break would do us all good."

"What about Chloe? And Simon, he'll be back for the summer."

"You're all big kids now. You know how to butter toast, don't you?"

"I don't mean that and you know it." Michael paused. "Anyway, I don't see how you can go."

Emma turned to face him; he looked bewildered.

"Why not?"

"Because you wouldn't dare. All that travelling on your own, much of it in the dark. You've never been further than Cornwall for twenty- five years. How could you cope?"

"I just would. I want to go."

"I don't know what's up with you. You're screwing us up, Emma."

As Michael shook his head and walked away; Emma remembered John saying those very words to her all those years ago in London. Funny, she thought philosophically, even over the same thing.

When Emma was at work the next day, sorting through veterinary case notes, Lorraine, a young vet nurse sidled up to Lorraine and sat on her desk, shyly swinging her legs. Lorraine was a pretty girl – the same age as Chloe – and often frequented the city's local pubs with Emma's daughter.

"So what's this then, eh? Florida?" said Lorraine.

"Well, hopefully."

"I was talking to Chloe in The Globe last night."

"Oh?" Emma picked up her coffee and drank nervously, grateful to have something to fidget with. Why had Lorraine joined her?

"Can I tell you something, Emma?" Lorraine lowered her voice and stared hard into Emma's eyes.

Emma felt most uncomfortable. "Of course. What is it, Lorraine?"

"I hope you don't mind me telling you this. Chloe was saying...er, about – Julian." She held a long silence. "And I'm adopted."

Emma was completely taken aback – at first she couldn't think what to say. Lorraine's admission humbled her and it made her feel in control, the comforter. Emma wanted to interrogate her.

"What has Chloe told you?" Emma spoke softly.

"That you found your son, wrote to him and got a letter back."

"Well, that sounds as if it's okay! But the letter was really a rejection."

"I bet he doesn't mean it, though."

"No?"

"No. I bet he's really happy you wrote. I'd give anything to have a letter from my natural mother. I mean, I love my parents and would never do anything to hurt them, so I can't try to trace my birth mother because they'd be devastated. But if I could just have a letter, telling me who I am, where I came from, you know, just to feel I have a past, an identity, and know I was still thought about. I'd probably do the same as Julian because it's too difficult to take further, but I think it's great what you did. I really do. He will have been pleased."

The other nurses, Sue and Debbie, wandered back into the main area preparing for animal surgery and further conversation was curtailed, which was perhaps a relief as neither knew now what to say. They exchanged a brief smile, and Emma lightly touched Lorraine's hand.

Chapter Thirteen

"I fly out to Miami on Friday 3rd July, then there's a connecting flight to Naples which should, if all goes according to plan, get me there for eight pm." Telling Katy this made it seem terrifyingly real.

"Brilliant! I'll be waiting for you, then it's a straightforward drive down to Everglades City. We'll be at my place before 9.30. You'll love it here, I've got a rather humble shack overlooking the Barron River – basic but beautiful."

"Oh Katy, I'm so excited! I haven't felt like this for years!"

"Are your family okay about you coming?"

"Well the kids are pretty independent now, though I guess Michael's a bit put out. But I think it'll do us good, Katy. And I really need to talk to you."

"Sure, we'll do plenty of that. We can just sit out here on the balcony every night and talk ourselves silly!" Katy laughed. Emma could hear a slight American drawl in her friend's voice. She sounded happy. "Hey! I know what I meant to ask you – did you ever get in touch with John? Last time we spoke, you said you were going to."

"No, no I haven't. I've been meaning to find him. I don't know, I feel a bit guilty, but I really want to." Emma paused reflectively for a moment. "Actually, I think I will. I'll dig him out the archives and tell you all about it when I come over. Oh…" her voice quietened to little more than a whisper, "here's Mike. I'll go now and give you another call in a couple of weeks. Bye."

"Great to hear from you! Bye!"

Michael put his briefcase on the table and went back into the hall. Sam bounded after him enthusiastically but was rebuked by a subdued voice cautioning him to "stay down and leave". Emma glanced curiously towards the door and saw Michael reappear with a bunch of flowers. "These are for you," he said clumsily. A strange embarrassed awkwardness filled the room.

Poor Michael, Emma thought. He thinks he's losing me and doesn't know why. She went up to her husband and kissed him on the cheek. "Thanks, they are really lovely. What a nice thing to do."

Michael shrugged. A helpless shrug. "Who were you on the phone to?" he asked.

"Katy. Just talking about holiday dates."

"Oh."

Emma placed the flowers in a vase. She stood with her back to him. He coughed, almost nervously, before continuing, "I thought you might like to go out for a meal tonight?"

Michael was a proud man, not given to weakness or grovelling. For him to display these acts of generous humility must mean he was seriously upset. He seemed to have no idea that Emma had been thrown into chaos by finding Julian and needed the break to take a step back and re-evaluate. He had no idea she'd been seeing a counsellor, nor that she'd got a letter back from Julian And he certainly didn't know about the letter from Mary Brandon. He just seemed to think that following years of stale marriage, Emma had fallen completely out of love with him.

The next morning Emma had three phone calls that she wanted to make once the house was empty. Two were to organisations Amanda Payne had given her: Adoption UK and the NPN, The Natural Parents' Network.

The third phone call was to find John.

Emma topped up the vase of flowers with fresh water. She felt sorry for Michael and knew she was giving him a hard time. Perhaps it would be better if she tried to explain things to him? Tell him about the letters? Reassure him but ask for his support? But she was so scared of his disapproval and criticism, she felt unable to share this part of her life with him.

Emma sensed that her reactions and emotions were evolving somehow. It was almost as if she had to work through feelings, revive and exorcise past memories, come to terms with loss and try to somehow accept Oliver's – no – Julian's, rejection of her. Oliver, she had decided, was hers. The precious memory of her baby. Julian was the man, another woman's son who had no part in Emma's life. In time, she hoped she would learn to move on, and then she'd be back to her old self again. Indeed, a better self with no hidden bits shoved into corners.

"Hello, I'm Emma Gray and I've been given your number by an adoption counsellor. I'm a birth mother who's found her son – well, not found exactly because he doesn't want to meet me, but I'm trying to find out how the adoptive mother feels in these situations, and the adoptee, and I wondered if Adoption UK could offer any information?"

The lady, Julia Warburton, was kind and responsive, she thanked Emma for her consideration and indicated she thought there may well be someone who would welcome a chat with Emma.

"I would need to ask her permission first, of course, but if it's all right with you, perhaps I could leave her your phone number?"

Emma was delighted, insisting any call be made during the day, but yes, she would love to hear from her. How kind she was, thought Emma, warming to Julia's open and accommodating acceptance.

The second phone call to the NPN was equally comforting.

"Yes of course, we'll send you our latest newsletter and if you feel you would like to join us, there's a small £5 donation we ask for, but I'm sure you'll find it very helpful…"

Great. Brilliant. So far so good. Now for John.

When she'd been toothcombing all the Brandon's in telephone directories for the North of England, she'd casually flicked back to the Austins in case John's name had somehow presented itself. But there had always been several 'J. Austin's and she had only been idly curious anyway. Now she wanted to find him in earnest. But where to start? The thought of wading through the world's supply of John Austins left Emma daunted. It could be infinitely more difficult than finding Julian.

But what about Paul? The Paul that had a bedsit in Heaton? Now, what was his surname? The more she tried to concentrate, the further away it went. Lateral thinking, that's what she'd do. She needed to potter around the house making beds, washing pots, ironing and it would come on its own accord eventually. Only half an hour later, wiping the ring off the sides of the bath, the name suddenly darted into her thoughts.

Kaufmann! That was it! Emma pelted downstairs three at a time, leaving beds half-made, swiping an increasingly neurotic Sam out of the way and raced into the kitchen. Kaufmann, Kaufmann, Kaufmann. She dialled 192 so quickly that she misdialled and had to start again. C'mon c'mon!

"Hello, name please?"

"Kaufmann in Newcastle."

"Could you spell that for me, please?"

"K a u f m a n n."

"And the address, please?"

"I don't actually have a precise address, but it's P. Kaufmann in New-castle-upon-Tyne." Emma prayed Paul still lived there. He'd loved New-castle and always said he'd never leave.

"Here's your number Caller…"

She'd done it! Oh, sometimes life could be so smooth.

She phoned but there was no answer. Well, it was eleven am on a Tuesday morning so she supposed he was at work. Impatience ate at her. Emma was not a person willing to wait more than five minutes once there was something she wanted to do or have. Evening phone calls would mean Michael was at home. So now what? Perhaps she could call from work? Her afternoon shifts didn't finish until six pm and although personal phone calls were not allowed, she would have to risk it. Waiting longer than today would be agony.

Emma was so busy scheming her next move that the telephone startled her.

"Hello?"

"Hello, Emma Gray?"

"Yes…"

"Oh hi, I'm Sandra Poole. Julia from Adoption UK has just been in touch with me and gave me your number. Is it okay to speak now?"

"Oh hello! Yes! How kind of you to phone me so quickly." Emma could hear a small child in the background. "Did she tell you – er, anything?"

"Yes, she did a bit." Sandra hesitated. "My son met his birth mother a couple of months ago."

"Oh, I see."

"Listen, I hate talking on the telephone, it's so impersonal. Is there any chance you could come over for coffee one day? I'm a bit tied up myself, child minding, but I'd love to meet you."

Emma kept glancing at the clock on the wall above the reception desk. The waiting room was still full of people and their pets and it looked as if she might end up working late, which suited her. A call to Michael would be legitimate. Paul's would be just one extra…

"Emma," called Mr Crossley, from his surgery, "I'm sorry but we seem to be running a bit behind schedule. I hope you can stay just another fifteen minutes or so – make any phone calls if you need to."

Great! The first to Michael was straightforward and she reassured him she'd be home as soon as they were finished. As she tapped out Paul Kaufmann's number it suddenly crossed her mind it might not be him at all, that it was feasible another P. Kaufmann existed. Emma could feel her heart thumping against her chest. A woman answered.

"Hello?"

"Hello, is Paul there please?"

"Yes, just hold on a moment I'll get him for you. Who's calling?"

"Emma. Emma Hargreaves." Wow! Was it really going to be as straightforward as this? She heard a muffled exclamation in the distance before an immediately familiar voice. How strange that voices never seem to change, she thought briefly.

"Emma? Oh, this is amazing! How wonderful to hear from you! After all these years… how the hell are you? Strangely enough, I was only talking to John about you the other day, remembering the 'good old days'!"

Emma could feel herself perspiring with excitement. "Listen," Emma kept her voice low, "I'm phoning from work. I've been wanting to get in touch with John again."

"Ah. He actually lives in down Folkestone now but give me your home number and I'll get him to give you a call – daytime, yes?"

"Yes please. That's really good of you." She gave him her number.

Emma almost skipped to her car after closing the practice and sang out loud all the way home. Another big "tidying up" step, though quite how or why she didn't understand. Once back, she threw her coat on the hall floor, went into the kitchen and saw Michael washing pots and, high on a long forgotten happiness, flung her arms around her husband's waist and squeezed him tightly.

"Love you," she said softly.

Michael turned round with soapy hands, clearly taken aback, but he cupped her face in wet bubbles and kissed her. "Love you, too."

The next morning, John rang.

Emma's mind was whizzing as she put down the phone. Her heart still racing, she heard the echo of John's words. How strange that almost thirty years could feel like no more than five minutes. So, married twice and now living with a new lover in Folkestone! Like Katy. But unlike Katy, John had three children, two from his first wife, one from his second. Well, four children altogether.

But it was great to hear from him. It helped emotionally too, almost like talking to Julian by proxy. And, of course, John was thrilled to hear about Julian – Oliver to John. He couldn't grasp the name Julian and referred to their son only as Oliver. "Good for you!" he had enthused on telling him she'd written to him. "He must be crazy to keep you at arms length. Maybe he's been indoctrinated into a pseudo sense of loyalty by stifling parents. I wonder if he's inherited my rugged blond good looks and intelligence?"

John laughed in the same superior, confident manner that had captivated Emma years ago. It was relief to joke about something that had brought so many tears; a relief to share talk of Oliver. John had gone on to suggest he "look him up" and "sort him out", but finding that approach rather insensitive, Emma had diverted his train of thought to present, everyday conversation. It was left that they keep in touch now, albeit discreetly. Phone numbers and addresses were exchanged as they tried to devise some plan of meeting.

Sandra Poole lived near Horningsea, about thirteen miles away. Her modern detached bungalow was situated on the far edge of a quaint old village with little thatched cottages.

"Emma? Hi! Do come in," Sandra looked about ten years older than Emma, but still very attractive, with that firm slim figure secured through childlessness. The house was cluttered with toys, and photographs adorned the walls with what Emma supposed were family, ranging in age from about six months to mid-twenties.

"I'm so glad you came! Whoops, mind that car, Steven, you'll skid on that if you're not careful. Excuse the mess," Sandra turned now to Emma, "I have three children on a regular basis, child minding, but Steven makes up for them all put together!"

Steven looked about two and a half. An edible, angel-faced scruff with shaggy blond hair and huge blue eyes. He wore denim dungarees with plastic cars sticking out of every conceivable pocket. Sandra scooped him up and rested him on her hip. "Little ragamuffin!" she laughed, tousling his blond mop. Emma threw him a companionable wink and he buried his reddening cheeks into Sandra's chest.

Fifteen minutes later, they sat drinking coffee. "So, what happened with your son?" queried Sandra kindly.

Emma was rather shocked that Sandra called him her son. Even she rarely allowed herself such indulgence. Warily, Emma told her story. It was difficult for her to talk about it to an adoptive mother; she felt defensive.

"Oh, he'll probably change his mind in time," said Sandra dismissively, "kids have to wade through a lot of conflicting feelings."

"Tell me about your son," said Emma.

"Well, my older son, Matthew, approached me one day saying he wanted to trace his natural mother. I helped him, of course. But it wasn't easy."

Emma nodded.

"The thing is," continued Sandra, "it all felt rather unfair. He's a lovely young man, loyal, caring and it seemed out of character for him to want to search for her. I thought we were all fine. It felt like a rejection of us as a family."

"How difficult," offered Emma. "But it isn't, is it?"

"No, not at all. I knew that intellectually, but I thought that as soon as he met his birth mother, I'd be second best. I was angry at the disruption and terrified over losing him. Yet if I didn't help him search, who would? It would have become secretive – much worse. And then, of course, he needed support. So despite my own fears, I felt obliged to be with him all the way."

"How would you have felt if it had been the other way round, the birth mother trying to find Matthew?"

Sandra leaned back in her chair and stared at the wall. "Angry, I guess. At the intrusion. Protective towards Matthew, too." Her eyes now rested on Emma. "I think I would have felt quite distrustful if Matthew's birth mother had sought him out. I'd perhaps find it threatening. Also I'd wonder how she'd found him, and then why."

Emma flushed uncomfortably. "But surely, it would feel reassuring for Matthew – or any other adopted person. Doesn't it go some way to making amends? At least if the birth mother makes the first move, it saves them from the risk of being rejected in their own searching. And they can always say no thank you, like Julian."

"I see your point, but the risk is still there. The biological mother can still reject a second time. Just because she's the one to initiate contact doesn't mean she won't abandon her child again, just as she did once before."

Emma felt furious at the insensitivity of the remark but kept quiet. She didn't want an argument. "We didn't have much choice, you know," she offered politely.

"No. No, I'm sorry. Of course you didn't. I understand that, but I'm thinking of the adoptee. He or she has to come first."

"Tell me what happened with Matthew," Emma decided this a safer approach. "Presumably he met his, er…?"

"Yes. Yes, last October. I wasn't there, they met at the hotel she'd travelled to for the reunion. I understand it went well. Matthew hasn't elaborated a great deal but I believe they rather liked one another. They exchanged photographs, Matthew has shown me a picture of her, she looks very nice. They have met twice since. He went to stay with her and her family just after Christmas and she visited him at his flat last month. She's much younger than me, of course." Sandra was trying to sound generously accommodating but was having difficulty. There was an edge to her voice.

"It's been hard for you?" asked Emma.

Sandra raised her eyebrows and rolled her eyes. "You think of all the years you've had bringing them up: the bonding, their childhood and schooling, those horrendous adolescent years – not to mention the humiliating procedure to adopt in the first place, and snap," she clicked her fingers, "they turn round and say 'Well, where's my mum?' When we had Matthew, we were assured there would never be any contact with the birth parents again, that he was our son and that we could consider him absolutely our own. Then in 1975, they decided to move the goal posts. No conferring, no apologies, no explanations. Just that all of a sudden, children over the age of eighteen now had the right of access to their original birth records, and that we, as good, loving adoptive parents, were supposed to support it. It wasn't on the cards at the beginning, but now it was. Tough if you didn't like it."

"And one day, Matthew decided to trace?"

"Yes."

"But has it changed your relationship with him?"

"Luckily for us, it improved things, if anything. Matthew seems more calm and at peace with himself now. He says he feels a more complete person and can understand himself better. And there is a half brother he gets on very well with – but it's been very hard for him. It unearthed as many questions as answers. He's needed us very much, and, as always, it's been me there to comfort him." Sandra took a deep breath and held a brief silence before continuing. "Even before he wanted to search, there was always that underlying dread that one day he'd want to, and it almost feels safer now, a relief, that it's happened – and we've survived. But the upheaval."

Emma felt heavy. What an ordeal. What had she done to Julian and his family? What had she done to her own? Julian would never have tried to trace her, that she knew, which made her acutely envious of Matthew's birth mother. How very, very lucky she was to have met her son – held him, no doubt. Hugged him. The envy lay leaden in her heart.

"How do you feel about Matthew's birth mother?"

Sandra fiddled nervously with a toy car. "I'm afraid I haven't much compassion for her. I don't think she has a moral right now to claim his affections. Sometimes loyalty and love are earned by dedication, not genetics. Personally I find it hard to accept that after all the years we've given to bringing up Matthew, she can expect a close bond with him."

Emma listened politely. There was a strong feeling of disapproval in Sandra's voice when she spoke of Matthew's birth mother which was quite different from her general manner.

"But of course, your mother," Sandra said smiling now, turning the tables, "what a wonderful woman. She must have suffered such private heartache, and keeping that newspaper clipping all those years – no doubt intending you to find it one day."

My mother? thought Emma, taken aback. Emma had never thought of her mother's feelings in all this. And keeping the newspaper cutting deliberately?

"How did she find out?" continued Sandra.

"Er, I really don't know. To this day I have no idea and I guess I never will." Emma felt confused recalling her mother's role.

"She was very good, wasn't she? To look after your baby for you to save you from bonding with him. What a wrench to let her first grandchild go. And then to find out where he'd gone and hold that secret all those years! And yet she selflessly kept that cutting for you to find after she'd died, allowing you the choice she denied herself."

Emma's thoughts slipped back. She visualized her mother, tried to remember those ten days of having Oliver before he was fostered, recalled that cry – the creaking gate, and lying in bed hearing the muffled movements of Mum tending her baby downstairs. Oh my God, poor Mum! She had never, ever considered her mother's grief. Her first grandson. What lonely grief she must have suffered. All Emma had done was dwell on her own. If Chloe was pregnant, and she nursed the baby, would she want to let it go? Never. Emma was exhausted, confused and overwhelmed. She wanted to go.

Gently the conversation turned towards more comfortable matters: Simon and Chloe, Michael's job, the small children Sandra looked after, even shopping at Tesco until eventually Emma decided it was time to leave.

"It's been great meeting you," said Emma. She stood up and Sandra also rose from her chair. They hugged briefly.

"All in the name of love. We have to love our children, and if that means letting go, well, so be it. I've learned that, if nothing else!" Sandra smiled, " I hope you meet your son one day, I really do."

Little Steven had been the perfect angel during the afternoon, playing industriously with his toy cars. Emma squatted down and kissed him. He grunted disapprovingly, wiped his face then beamed back at her. She imagined Oliver at two and a half, and ruffled his hair.

As Emma drove away, she reflected on everything that had been said that afternoon. The biggest disturbance was the thought of her mother's grief at losing Oliver. Why hadn't she thought of that before? She remembered now the final closing of that front door when they'd come to take him away and her mum's strangled moan. How selfish had she been? To what ends had her mother gone to trace her grandson's whereabouts? It must have been virtually impossible, but she'd done it. Had she ever meant to tell Emma, or prayed that on her death, Emma would find that cutting?

The blocks were crumbling, dissolving now for Emma. She could just recall her past, touch it, feel it, by simply remembering. But her mum. Poor Mum. Poor Mum! Tears started to roll down Emma's cheeks. Oh, why didn't I think? If only now they could be together, talk, cuddle, get it all out in the open. How stupid to have pretended it had all never happened. Emma was now working through it, freeing blocked emotions - but her mother? She took that heartache to the grave with her. I gave her that pain, Emma now realized. Oh Mum, I'm sorry, I'm so, so sorry...

Emma could hardly see out the car window for tears blurring her vision. She was aware of her own choking cry, consumed with sorrow, not for herself but her mother. "Mum! Mum, I love you!"

Suddenly, the car was filled with a presence.

That's all you could call it. A presence. Goose pimples waved over Emma from the top of her head to the tips of her toes. She froze, her tears arrested in the icy chill, yet she felt blanketed with love, with euphoria.

"Mum?"

"Sshh sshh, my wee bairn. It's all right, there there."

"MUM?"

But it was gone. She was gone. Emma flung her head round to the backseat, almost swerving into the roadside – but of course no-one was there. Anyway, the voice hadn't come from the back seat. It had been in her head – yet real. Her mum had spoken to her.

Emma wiped her eyes and nose with the back of her hand. She smiled. A strange, overwhelming sense of peace flooded over her.

"Thanks, Mum."

Chapter Fourteen

Time to talk.

Emma had drunk over half a bottle of Chardonnay before she felt brave enough to say anything, and she was still clear headed. Michael hadn't finished his first glass yet.

"You know," Emma's voice sounded to her as if it didn't belong to her, " you've never ever asked me about Julian." There. It was out. A clumsy attempt at communicating. Emma's hands were trembling. She hid them under the table so that he couldn't see.

"Who's Julian?"

"Julian – Oliver, the baby."

"Oh, that. Is there anything to ask?" His voice tightened.

"I thought you might wonder if I'd ever heard from him. Might care how I feel about it."

Michael was confused, not sure what was being asked of him, and bristled noticeably. "I presumed you'd tell me anything you wanted me to know."

"Shall I tell you now?"

"If you like."

Michael obviously didn't like, but Emma had decided to tell him. She knew she had deceived her husband badly, but amends could now only be made by wading forward and talking about it. "I wish you'd show more interest and understanding."

"What's brought all this on all of a sudden?" Michael refilled his glass aggressively, spilling a few drops onto the table. He didn't refill Emma's.

"All of a sudden? Oh Mike, I've been in total mourning for the last six months! I've been having counselling trying to work through a load of post traumatic stress – and you say 'all of a sudden'!"

Post traumatic stress was a new term Emma had learned from the Natural Parents' Network newsletter, relating to the process of delayed grief. Michael sighed. He was shocked to hear Emma talk about "counselling" and "mourning".

"I didn't think you were so close to your mother."

"Not my mother! Oliver!" She wanted to call him Oliver.

"Oh, we're back to that, are we?"

"Why are you so blocked on all this?"

"Me blocked? It's not my problem!"

"Well ask me then. Ask me about things. – if I heard from Julian."

Michael ran his hand through his hair. "What do you want me to know?"

"I don't necessarily want you to know, I want you to ask."

"Okay. Have you heard from Julian?"

"Yes."

Emma thought she saw a flicker of reaction.

"When?"

"Months ago."

"Well, what do you want me to ask now?"

"Don't you want to know what he said?"

"Not really. I think you know my feelings about all this." He stood up and took their plates to the kitchen sink.

"If you don't share this with me, you'll lose me." Emma shocked herself with this announcement.

"I don't think that's a reasonable ultimatum, Emma." Michael poured himself another glass of wine.

"All I want, please, is your support."

"I'm sorry, Emma. I cannot support what you're doing. I think it's basically wrong, interfering in other people's private lives. Okay, you had a baby and I appreciate it must have been difficult, but that child was given up for adoption. You can't start meddling with the past. For God's sake, you've got two great kids – and, if you remember, a good husband. Leave well alone and start thinking about us."

"You don't understand! All this 'basically wrong' crap is what's killing me. I had all that years ago. That's why I'm so screwed up over it now. And all you're doing is protecting yourself. Why should you care about Mrs Brandon? You sound a paragon of virtue but you're just as fucking jealous and insecure as the rest of us."

"What *did* Julian say?"

"That he doesn't want to know."

"Well there you are." Michael shrugged his shoulders. "I'm taking the dog out for a walk."

Emma got the biggest suitcase from the attic and dusted it down. She was going in four weeks and had begun to plan what she was taking. She also needed to organize domestic matters: stock the freezer up, buy in household items such as soap powder and loo roll, not that Michael and Chloe couldn't shop – but she'd stock up where she could, get the spare bedroom ready for Simon. Then she herself needed insect repellent, suntan cream, a month's supply of paracetamol, although admittedly her headaches were quite infrequent now, and she must go and visit Dad.

She was quite looking forward to going to Newcastle as she'd decided to call in on Paul.

Idly scanning through the wardrobe, deciding what she might take, she felt excited and afraid. It was more than just travelling alone, more than a month in America, more than seeing Katy again, it was a trial separation from Michael. Did she want their marriage to end? Was there no love left? Their problems couldn't all stem from her looking for Oliver.

The drive to Newcastle was particularly stressful. For a start she had a hangover, then a lorry had jack-knifed at Scotch Corner causing a huge traffic hold up. It took over four hours to reach Boulter Street. Fortunately, Jack looked good, and seemed to be coping well.

"If I went out tonight, Dad, would you mind?"

"Out, love? No, of course I wouldn't, but where are you going?"

"There's an old friend from yonks ago. I'd like to call on him. Actually, can I use the phone please, Dad?"

"You go ahead, my love. That sounds nice for you."

Paul insisted he collect her and promised to drop her back later as it would be too difficult for her to find his place. He remembered her parents' house and looked forward to seeing her and his wife would be delighted to lay on a light meal. He also warned Emma that they had three rather boisterous children, two dogs and a cat.

"So you're still in touch with John, then?" asked Emma twisting the spaghetti adeptly round her fork. Paul looked well, broader than his student years but still the same full head of hair and easy smile. Timothy, his six-year-old son, had resorted to sucking his dinner, thread at a time.

"Timothy! Eat properly now! Yes, we keep in touch. Obviously with him living in Folkestone we don't get together very often. Have you seen him lately, Emma?"

"I haven't seen him since 1968. He phoned me at home a few weeks ago after I'd sought you out the archives," Emma grinned at Paul. "Thanks for that. It was really weird because in a way, it seemed more like five minutes than nearly thirty years."

"1968! Wow, Emma! I've got a spare room upstairs for a packet of fags..." Paul laughed while his wife looked on with a small, confused smile. "I tell you what," Paul continued, "after dinner we'll phone him up – I'll phone him and put you on the line as a surprise."

Emma felt the colour come into her cheeks. This was borderline disloyal – but fun. After the meal, Emma helped Paul's wife, Caroline, clear away the pots while Paul put Timothy to bed and encouraged the other two to watch television in their playroom.

Caroline put the kettle on for coffee which disappointed Emma because she felt she needed a glass of something strong right now. Then Paul settled himself next to the phone and tapped the line of digits. "Hi mate! It's me, Paul. How are you doing?"

A lighthearted, easy conversation ensued, then Paul stopped briefly and said he had someone there who wanted to speak to him, then he passed Emma the receiver, nodded to Caroline and they both left the room, leaving Emma alone.

"Hello John, it's Emma."

Fifteen minutes later, Emma replaced the receiver. Paul re-entered, and seeing her flushed appearance smiled sensitively.

"Okay?" he asked.

"He's coming up. He's leaving now, stopping off overnight in the Midlands and expects to be here tomorrow lunchtime," Emma could hear the shakiness in her own voice. "Oh God, Paul, I haven't seen him for so many years…"

"Crikey, he must be keen!" Caroline stood in the doorway carrying a tray of coffee.

Emma couldn't bear it. "Can I have something stronger please, Paul? Dry martini, gin and tonic – anything."

Jack knew things must be wrong at home. A wife didn't desert her family for a month unless something was wrong. Things had changed these days, he knew that, but nevertheless, it wasn't right. Still, it was none of his business so he kept quiet. But now Emma had said she would be out all afternoon and evening. He was hardly seeing anything of her.

"No love, if that's what you want," he'd said dejectedly.

"I tell you what, I'll stay till tomorrow evening and drive down late, then we can have more time together." Blow the dark, she thought. If I can survive Miami airport alone, I'll manage the A1 in pitch black.

"Won't Michael be waiting for you?"

"Oh, he'll cope for another few hours, then we can have a Sunday roast together, yes?"

Jack smiled at his daughter, appeased. She did seem more independent these days.

Emma wished she had something more exciting to wear but had only travelled up with jeans and two tee-shirts. Nevertheless, her reflection showed a new sparkle and spirit that belied her years. She tried to quell disloyal fantasies of the memory of her and John's youthful passion. She wondered what he looked like now.

Paul picked her up at midday saying John was already there and was most excited to be seeing Emma. "He's in good form," winked Paul, but she didn't know what he meant by that.

Emma felt as nervous as a teenager on her first date. This is stupid, she thought, arguing with her conscience that there was nothing wrong in seeing an old boyfriend for a chat.

"Hi."

John stood in the lounge, his back to the fireplace, his hands locked behind him. She knew him; she didn't know him. The face was familiar; it was different. He looked older than she imagined, drawn, tense, a muscle in his cheek twitched nervously as he smiled.

"Hello." They didn't touch. Paul breezed off to make coffee and left them in the living room alone.

"So, how's life…?" The same voice. His blond hair, longer than in his youth and combed back, was dulled; snow white strands streaked the temples. The blue eyes fixed on her, surrounded by deep creases, his mouth framed with lines and jaw somewhat heavier with a double chin. A thickened waistline forced the belt of his trousers below his stomach. The Nordic god was now an overweight middle-aged Nordic god. She wanted desperately to find his face attractive, to feel a surge of attraction – but nothing.

"Fine," she said simply. He was as busy as her, staring. Paul re-emerged with two coffees, smiled and left the room again. Gingerly, they sat down next to each other on the settee to drink their coffee and began awkwardly recapping a quarter of a century's separate ways.

"And so next it's Florida for a month," Emma paused. As a boy, John dominated her with strong opinions; now it was Emma who felt in control, the more self assured. He spoke with the same confident arrogance, but he came across as egotistic, immature.

"So what's this about Oliver?" John asked eventually, leaning back with both arms stretched behind his head. A button came undone on his shirt.

Emma related the short chain of events.

"Perhaps I could write to him?" he suggested.

"Well, I can't stop you but I'd rather you didn't, for his sake. If he wanted to get in touch, he knows where I am."

John relaxed his arms and rested his hands on his thighs. Emma looked at his hands, his fingers, now quite plump. It suddenly seemed an intimate part of him, full of memories. An image of them making love came into her mind.

"I just thought perhaps you being his mother might come over as too intense," he said. "I'm not so emotional. I could appeal to his sense of curiosity without frightening him off."

"Maybe." She half wanted John to make contact, yet knew she'd be jealous if he did. Also, his attitude could come over as demanding. He would expect Julian to respond and have no time for hesitation. And what if Mike got wind that John was in on the scene again. "Perhaps when I get back from America we can see?"

"Sure." John grinned. "I'd like to see him myself. Should be a bit of all right, eh? My brains and your good looks." Emma nearly challenged the remark but didn't bother. Instead, she quizzed him about his marriages, his latest girlfriend, his children. He replied in quips that had no substance, sentences that she would once have considered intellectual and satirical came over as boring. She wondered if he lacked feeling or just pretended to. After an hour or so, their conversation petered to an end and Emma hoped he didn't feel he'd wasted his time travelling all that distance to meet her.

When Paul prepared to drive her back to Boulter Street, Emma and John hesitated with their farewells, unsure as to how to say goodbye. Shallow promises were made for continued contact, he reassured her that he would "sort this kid out" if nothing further was heard. Emma knew they wouldn't be in touch again.

That night in bed, Emma felt a sense of relief. It had been a tidy accomplishment seeing John. Another building block in the healing process. There had been no spare room for a packet of cigarettes, and no desire.

Chapter Fifteen

Simon came home to Emma's suitcase in the hall. In fact the house was bedlam. He dumped his guitar, rucksack and bin liner full of dirty washing in the kitchen.

Michael had offered to drive Emma down to Heathrow the next day, Friday. The flight was due to depart at six pm, but she'd need to be there for three to check in in good time. It was unbelievably hot in England and Emma wondered how she'd cope with the even greater heat in Florida. They were all on top of each other at home, with bags and baggage, boxes and books everywhere. Bad timing really to have one come and one go within forty-eight hours of each other.

Michael wandered around the house restlessly. He seemed the only one without direction. "Maybe we can both go somewhere next year?" he suggested lamely. He sat at the kitchen table watching his wife re-check the contents of her shoulder bag. The crossword lay in front of him, untouched.

"Yes, that would be good," said Emma. "Look after Sam, won't you, Chloe?"

"I will, Mum. Don't you worry about a thing."

"And Simon – don't expect your sister to cook your meals!"

Emma hugged each one in turn, long and hard; tears welled up in her eyes but neither of the children seemed unduly moved.

"Have fun," they chorused.

Emma squatted down to cuddle Sam, scooping her finger down the abrupt tilt of his blunt nose, making him sneeze in disapproval.

"Ready?" asked Michael. "I've got everything in the car."

Emma had never been to Heathrow before. It seemed like a town in itself. She was glad to have Michael with her.

Michael parked up on the roof car park, got all Emma's luggage out the boot and they made their way to terminal four. They were quiet, just Michael protectively checking her flight details every now and again. Got your passport? Boarding pass? You know it's American Eagle at Miami? Get your suitcase off the carousel before taking the connecting flight. Katy knows what time you'll be arriving?

Time to board. They clung together, their closeness was an unspoken shock to them both. As she softly pulled away, they held each other's gaze, both moved.

"Love you, Michael."

"Love you, too."

And she was gone. Michael turned away to head towards the car park. It was a beautiful day. Clear blue sky. He stayed on the roof car park watching the planes land and take-off and decided to wait until Emma's plane left. Eventually, the 747 to Miami International taxied to hold, put on full power, cruised down the runway building up speed and took off, easing its weight effortlessly into the skies.

Once it was out of sight, Michael got in his car, rested his arms over the steering wheel, laid his head onto his hands and burst into tears.

Eight hours later, the plane touched down in Miami. Overwhelmed, disorientated yet high with excitement, Emma filed along with the hundreds of other passengers, queuing for passport clearance and talking to anyone near her, for reassurance. It was early evening, still light. Emma gazed around the bustling crowds trying to guess where people had come from. There were cowboy hats, beautiful girls, deeply tanned bodies, young travellers, middle-aged couples in suits. Once through customs, Emma kept close to familiar faces, but after collecting her baggage she was on her own. She found her way to the correct waiting area for the connecting flight to Naples.

At 7.15 she boarded the small aircraft to Naples, flying over Miami and then what looked like, from the air, uninhabited green swampy land. It was just getting dark when they landed, Emma collected her suitcase and hand luggage and, following other passengers, walked straight ahead to the arrivals terminal.

"EMMA!"

"KATY!"

Emma burst into tears. Maybe it was tiredness, relief, jet lag, all mingled with the sheer delight of finding her old soul mate again after all those years.

They embraced each other tightly, then both stood back to look each other up and down.

"You sure look great!" grinned Katy.

Emma sniffed and wiped her eyes, fascinated with Katy's American twang. "So do you, and as skinny as ever, you bitch!"

They walked through some automatic doors into a car park. Although it was already dark, it felt like walking into a sauna.

"You stay here with your baggage and I'll bring the car over. Won't be a tic!"

Palm trees swayed in the shadows of the hot, dark night. A stretch limousine cruised by, stopping to pick up an elderly couple who Emma recognized as having been on her connecting flight. She glanced at her watch, adjusted it to local time. In England it would still be fairly light at this time of night. What was the time now in England? About 1.30 am. Michael would be in bed fast asleep. She thought of their last hug and now of him in bed without her, and wondered if a month apart was going to feel a long, long time.

A dilapidated large brown Chevrolet pulled up in front of her. Katy got out and piled Emma's luggage into the boot. "Okay? Right, let's go!"

Emma sank back in her seat, exhaustion washing over her, safe now in the competent and assured comradeship of Katy. She'd made it. Easy peasy lemon squeezy. A few glasses of wine and a little chat would just round off the day, then crash out until tomorrow.

Once on the U.S.41 or Tamiami Trail, they continued south for just under an hour. It was too dark to see much out the window, although Katy interjected with reference points and information en route: the Collier Seminole State Park, Marco island, mangrove swamps, alligator infested waters…

Katy turned right at a sign which said Everglades City. Within five minutes, she peeled into what looked like a caravan site. Emma sat upright, craning now through the car window, rather confused.

"Just round here," explained Katy, and finally drew up outside a large mobile shack, rather more isolated from the other huge American caravans, hook ups and mobile homes. "Not exactly the Hilton," she added, "but you'll grow to love it."

Emma got out the car and stretched. The Barron River twinkled gently under the stars, stillness and peace blanketing the warm night. Inside, Katy's home was humble and compact, yet with every facility – even a jacuzzi. There was a balcony adorned with sun loungers, low wicker table, easy cane chairs and barbecue set all directly overlooking the Barron River. Emma flopped onto a lounger.

"Rip Jaw will be here to greet you in the morning," grinned Katy.

"Rip Jaw?"

"We have a regular 'gator come by and bask over there on that embankment."

Emma craned to see beyond the water's edge but it was too dark.

"Oh dear, is that safe?"

"Well, I suggest you don't go swimming – but he won't come and get you! We have pelicans here, too, they come and perch on the riverside poles. Oh Emma, there's so much to show you!" Katy laughed. It made Emma feel happy inside. Here she was at long last, the other side of the world! Emma licked her dry lips. Dare she ask for a glass of something?

"Now let me get you a drink. You must be parched from all that flying." She went to the fridge and opened the door. Emma was drooling in anticipation. "I've got mineral water – or how about cranberry and apple juice? That's really refreshing. Or would you simply prefer an English cup of tea?'"

Oh dear.

"You've not any wine or martini, have you?" Emma asked sheepishly.

"Er, no. Sorry. I don't drink. I could maybe get some from the General Store," Katy glanced at her watch, "although I think they're closed now." Katy looked at Emma uncomfortably.

"Oh no, it doesn't matter," lied Emma. "Tea would be lovely."

The next day, Katy and Emma relaxed on the balcony, watching fishing boats, pelicans – and, indeed, Rip Jaw. They would leave journeying around for at least a day or two. The heat soared up into the nineties, but air conditioning rendered it comfortable. Emma phoned home to say she had arrived safely. She could hear the dog in the background noisily slurping water from his bowl. Then in the evening, after several glasses of cranberry and apple juice, Katy and Emma began to peel back the layers of privacy, edging slowly and cautiously into each other's past.

"So tell me all about Oliver," invited Katy softly.

Emma looked at her friend and noticed the lined furrow of her brow beneath the grey streaked fringe. Deeply tanned and still strikingly attractive, years in the hot sun had nevertheless weathered her complexion. Beneath her easy smile lay a sensitive, perhaps troubled, maturity.

"It all started when my mother died..." began Emma.

Twenty minutes of revelations later, she leaned back in the wicker chair. "And that's it really. That's where I'm at."

"Do you regret it?" asked Katy now.

"Regret giving him up or trying to find him again?"

"Well, I meant trying to find him – but okay, both then."

Emma stared out into the blackness of the Barron River, watching the dancing reflection of stars on the water. "I don't know. I don't know the answer to either."

"Mind you, think what a lousy mother you'd have made back in the sixties!"

"What do you mean?" protested Emma.

"Well, you were so young and easily led. Into drugs and all that hippie crap. Remember how you used to talk? All that 'wow man' and 'really cool' stuff."

Emma felt wounded. "But that's because of what happened! If I'd kept Oliver it might have been different."

"You'd never have got off the poverty wheel," Katy looked apologetic now. "There was absolutely no financial help in those days, you would never have found work as an unmarried mother and it would have crippled your mum and dad. Anyway, Oliver's probably been happiest with his adoptive family. He would have had a good home, a respectable upbringing and no doubt been loved by devoted parents. I guess all you can say is how lucky you are."

"Lucky?"

"Yes. You've learned he's well and alive and given him this wonderful opportunity to contact you if he ever wants to."

"You make it seem as if I should be grateful. Just like all those do-gooders did years ago!" She paused, "Oh Katy, I just love him so much. So much."

"I'm sorry," Katy placed a hand over Emma's. "I guess it's hard for me to understand. Crikey, have you been like this for all these years?"

"Well, no," Emma lowered her voice, "Funnily enough, I've always thought I was heartless. I used to think about him constantly, but without pain. Like it was a dead bit. I never really cried over him until recently. It's weird. I guess it got shoved down. Since I've really got into finding him, it's been like the dam walls have burst. And I still have this awful guilt thing even now."

Katy nodded, trying to understand. "I'm sure you'll feel better in time. Perhaps it would have been better left alone?"

"I don't know. I go round in circles. I know I'm upset, and I admit it's causing me more heartache than I've ever had, and I'm really really sorry for upsetting...others," Emma didn't dare tell Katy about the letter from Mary Brandon, "but I still feel better in a way for it. Crazy isn't it? Like digging out and unblocking an old rotten lump of something stuck." Emma sniffed through her tears and giggled at the description. "It just hurts shifting it, that's all."

Katy laughed too, keen to diffuse Emma's pain. "Hey! And what about John, then? C'mon, tell us all...!"

Emma snuggled down into her wicker chair and tucked her legs beneath her and began her story. Their conversation eventually started to dwindle with sleepiness. Katy had only given the skimpiest details of her own past, preferring to reflect and listen to Emma, but in some ways, Emma felt Katy hadn't really been able to understand her. Perhaps because she'd chosen not to have any children herself she wasn't particularly maternal.

"Anyway, bed time I think!" Emma stood up and yawned. Tiredness without alcohol was becoming rather pleasant. "Thanks for listening to me going on, Katy."

Katy smiled. "I know it's difficult, but honestly, still try and think of yourself as lucky to have created life." Her expression became reflective. "I'd swap."

Emma looked at Katy, surprised. "Swap? Why? You've got it made here! It's beautiful! Wildlife, sunshine, independence, friends."

"It's not what I wanted though."

"No?" Emma looked quizzically at her friend and noticed her biting her bottom lip.

"Nah," she tossed her head back dismissively, making light of it now. "I wanted my first marriage to work. And then my second. I wanted kids."

"Well, why didn't you then?"

Katy stared at her friend, pausing before taking a deep breath. "Can't have them, can I? I'm infertile."

That night in bed, Emma thought about Michael. She was relieved to find she missed him and worried about having left him alone. She wondered if Margaret was "popping in" to see if there was anything he needed. Maybe he wouldn't want her back. Her thoughts turned to Katy. Why couldn't she have children? Why hadn't Katy adopted a baby?

Before setting off the next morning for a visit to an Indian village, Emma phoned home. "Michael? It's me. How's things?"

"Hello! Oh so so. Bit chaotic. How are you?" Emma could hear the television on in the background. She pictured him relaxing in front of the news. She felt a long way away.

"Great! It's really good here – the wildlife is amazing. I've seen loads of alligators and beautiful birds. And it's so hot! Katy and I are getting on really well, we're travelling down the Florida Keys today…" Emma lowered her voice softly, "but I miss you Michael. I've been thinking of you."

"Good. Can't have you enjoying yourself and forgetting all about me. So you'll come back then?"

"Yes please, if you'll have me." Katy breezed by behind her with a small rucksack. She would have said more, but Katy's proximity inhibited her, "And how are Simon and Chloe and Sam?"

"Apart from Simon eating everything, Chloe trailing clothes everywhere and Sam tramping mud over the lounge carpet – fine."

"And work? Any word from my dad? Post?"

"Work's good, a few orders from Hollard's. Nothing from your dad. There's an airmail letter, I think from Steven. One other hand written envelope but mainly circulars and rubbish."

"Thanks. I wonder who the hand written one's from? Can you see a postmark?"

"Hang on, I'll just look…"

Emma waited briefly, listening to the movement of paper.

"Peterborough," he said. "Mean anything to you?"

Peterborough. Mary Brandon. Oh no.

"No," Emma lied. "No, nothing. Can't be important."

"You're quiet," observed Katy, "everything all right at home?"

For a moment, Emma held back but she took a deep breath and told Katy. "Mike says there's a letter for me from Peterborough."

"So?"

"That'll be Mrs Brandon, Julian – Oliver's mother."

"You weren't expecting to hear from her?"

"No way. Not after that last one."

"The last one? You never said anything about this, did you?"

Emma explained.

"Mmm. So why do you think she would be writing again?"

"God knows."

"You must get Michael to open it and read it out for you."

"I can't do that!"

"I reckon it might be best out in the open."

Katy saw a sign for Key Largo. "We'll stop there and get a room at the Hungry Pelican." She paused. "It would give Michael a part in it all, too."

Emma shuddered at the thought.

Later that night, they sat on the jetty overlooking the Florida Bay. Little fishing boats bobbed up and down while flocks of pelicans scoured the water's edge for morsels of fish. Neither Emma nor Katy spoke. The large red sun began to sink, creating a golden reflection on the sea.

"Shall we turn in?" yawned Katy.

Slowly, they ambled back to their room, slipped into bed and turned off the light.

"Katy…" breathed Emma softly. "Why can't you have children?"

"Blocked fallopian tubes."

"Can't they 'unblock' them?"

"Not in my case."

"I'm sorry."

"I had a barrage of tests, x-rays, and other treatments but they couldn't help."

"That's awful. I had no idea. Did you consider adoption?"

"We started the process, Alan and I," Katy's voice was flat. "But it's a shitty ordeal. They all but wanted to know what position you did it in. It was so humiliating, the questions, we felt we weren't good enough. And I realized in the end I couldn't adopt. I couldn't do it. I didn't want someone else's baby. It had to be mine or nothing."

"And Alan?"

"He left me." She paused. "Now I've dumped all that on you, promise to phone Michael and ask about that letter?"

"Oh Katy!"

"Promise?"

"Okay. Promise."

"You know that letter I got? The one with the Peterborough postmark?"

"Er, Peterborough? Oh yes."

"Would you open it for me please and read it out?"

There. She'd said it.

"Sure," he sounded confused, "hang on a minute." She heard him put the receiver down. "Here we are," he said at last. "Got it. Do you know who it's from?"

"I might." She could hear the rustle as he opened the contents. She was almost wretching with anxiety.

"'*Dear Emma,*' Michael coughed before continuing. Emma sat down. She wondered if he could hear her heart thumping on the other end of the line.

> *I trust this letter finds you well and I hope you don't mind me writing to*
> *you after all this time. As you will no doubt notice from the above address,*
> *I have moved back to my home town…*

Eh? Not Mary Brandon.

"Stop a minute, Michael. Could you just go to the end and see who it's from?

"Er, whoops – a couple of photos have just fallen out." An interminable pause. Michael seemed to be bending down to pick something up. Emma had stopped breathing. Everything was swimming. "Here we are, *Yours, Julian.*"

"Calm down, Emma! You'll wear a hole in the carpet!"

"I can't believe it. I can't believe it! He wrote! Michael said he looked quite tall on the photo. He's married. Oh Katy, I love him! I love him! I don't know how, but I do."

It was that same elation she'd felt after the birth, when she'd boasted to another new young mum in the ward that she'd just had a son. The midwife had told her to shut up. But now, that same euphoria. Emma continued to pace up and down.

"Michael was okay…he asked me if he could be with me if I met him. Do you believe that? He really seemed okay. This is all I could ever ask for in the world!" Emma flung outstretched arms to the ceiling and cast her eyes upwards. "I've found him; now I've finally found him and Michael is behind me."

She had been ready to drop it, prepared to put it behind her, and now this. She shook her head in disbelief.

"Don't expect too much, Emma. Don't raise your hopes too high. Julian only said '*maybe someday…*'" Katy cautioned.

"I know. I know. It's okay, don't worry for me. It won't be the same for him. I understand that." Emma's face was radiant. She beamed, seeing nothing but a dream come true. "I still feel I could eat him, though," she added.

Emma made Katy and herself a cup of tea. She couldn't eat breakfast. She couldn't drink her tea.

Katy shook her head despairingly. Emma's reaction seemed over the top. It was unhealthy, obsessive. "Emma, slow down a bit. You're like a runaway train."

"No I'm not. I'm perfectly calm and rational."

"Ahem!" coughed Katy derisively, raising her eyebrows.

"I know what you're thinking. You think I've flipped. I haven't. Not at all. Don't you see? It's not just me I'm thrilled for. But it means he's interested, curious, cares a bit about where he came from."

"Don't forget Michael."

"I won't. He comes first now, all the way down the line. I shall pamper him to death from now on."

Chapter Sixteen

The 747 began its descent over north Wales. The weather looked dull and overcast but Emma didn't care.

The plane landed at eight am. Dizzy with exhaustion and impatience, she bolted through customs and pushed her baggage trolley at road rage speed towards the arrival terminal. Four weeks ago, she had landed at Naples to the affectionate welcome of Katy. Now she was back.

Michael! And he was there, their arms were thrown around each other tightly. Rocking, squeezing, silent. He kissed her hair and she buried her nose into his neck. As if in a dream, she let Michael push the trolley, then he told her to wait whilst he got the car and put her luggage in the boot. Before driving off, he laid his hand on hers and squeezed it. His eyes were hungry. Emma smiled, tears streaming down her face.

"Nice to have you back," he said.

The journey back to Cambridge was strained with suspense, but their conversation remained light, as if everything was on hold for the time being. The children were fine, Sam was okay, Jack had had a fall but no, nothing broken and he was well again now. Yes, Emma had had a wonderful time. She didn't ask about the letter from Julian...she was saving that for later. Relaxed, secure in Michael's care, she drifted in and out of their conversation. By early lunch-time, they pulled into the drive of their home and she awoke excited. The house seemed alien for a moment. She wandered through into the kitchen; it had been cleaned recently although Emma noticed tell-tale signs of neglect. The plants were dry and leggy, but she was home. Somewhere in this house there was a letter from Julian, and photos of him. But that would wait.

Emma turned to Michael who was staring at her, waiting.

"Where are Simon and Chloe?"

"I've given them one and six pence to go and play in the park with Sam." He grinned, walked over to Emma, took her by the hand and led her up to their bedroom. Then he closed the door and locked it.

"Where's Mum?" exploded Chloe two hours later, rushing through the back door.

"Fast asleep," said Michael. "We'll wake her in a bit."

Simon removed Sam's lead and watched the dog leave muddy prints all over the kitchen floor. Michael shook his head despairingly.

But Emma heard their return and came downstairs to be with her family. She gave each of them small presents and related stories of alligators, venomous snakes, prolific bird life, manatee and hot, hot sun. Before long she was wilting again, and so desperate now to see that letter. "Would you mind, folks, if I called it a day?" yawned Emma.

"Sure, that's fine," said Michael. "Anything I can get you?"

"I wonder if you'd just look in on me in a few minutes, Michael?"

"Sure."

He sat on the edge of the bed, Emma lay tucked up under the duvet.

"Tired?"

Pause. Deep breath. Why was this so difficult? "A bit. I wonder why?!" She rolled onto her back and grinned at him before adding what she hoped sounded like an afterthought, "Oh, that letter Michael, can I see it?"

"What letter?"

"The one from Julian."

"Oh of course! Sure, I'll get it."

Michael returned with the envelope. "Do you want me to leave you alone?"

Yes no yes no.

"No, stay, please."

Dear Emma,

I trust this letter finds you well and I hope you don't mind me writing to you after all this time. As you will no doubt notice from the above address, I have moved back to my home town.

Becci (my wife) is expecting our first child in January and it seemed the right time to settle down permanently. I have been lucky enough to secure a good post with Ambray Graphics as a consultant design engineer and I like to think the future looks promising.

Although my last letter spoke of us not making further contact, I feel now that the dust has settled, it is something I would like to keep an open mind on. Also, I have some questions concerning my biological background. If you consider it appropriate and are comfortable with the idea, I would also like to know of the father's whereabouts.

I enclose a couple of photos of myself and Becci (I'm the one on the left!). Maybe someday we can look forward to meeting one another but for now, I look forward to hearing from you if you feel you would like to write anytime, as I hope you do.

Best wishes to you and your family,

Yours,

Julian

The photo showed a blond haired young man, square jaw, slightly built with a composed, intelligent smile that reminded her of John. Becci was a petite, dark and pretty girl. Both of them were strangers. She stared at Julian, waiting for something to click – but it didn't. She didn't know him at all.

"He's struggled a bit, hasn't he?" smiled Michael.

"What do you mean?" There was no hint of criticism in Emma's voice, just open curiosity.

"He sounds sort of stiff, like trying to be correct."

"Yes," smiled Emma affectionately. "How do you feel about it now?"

Michael shrugged his shoulders. "I don't know. Something about him, Julian, seems real and I feel, sort of - I know this sounds silly, but paternal. I'm not sure about the John bit, though."

Emma nodded. Softly softly catchee monkey. They were talking. "You know you have absolutely nothing to worry about, don't you?" She hadn't told Michael she'd met John in Newcastle and the time was hardly right now. Perhaps later. Perhaps not.

"Sure. But imagine it the other way round, if I started calling up old flames."

"Yes, I understand." Leave that for a bit. "But you'd be okay if I wrote to Julian?"

"Of course I would."

"Will you help me write it? I'd like to think we can be together on this. That matters to me more than anything."

"I'm sorry. I've not been very good, have I? I guess you were right when you accused me of being insecure and jealous, but it's been a hell of a shock, you know."

"It must have been, Michael. I know I should have said before we got married."

"I didn't trust you, I didn't know what was going to happen. I cut myself out of it then felt excluded."

"And I cut you out of it, too. We should have talked but neither of us felt we could. But we are the most important thing. Can you trust me now?"

Michael flopped on the bed next to his wife. Evening sunlight filtered through the closed curtains. Muted noises drifted up from the television and children downstairs, traffic sounds in the distance and the footfalls of passers-by.

By October, Simon was back at Brighton University and Chloe had started at Loughborough College of Art and Design. Emma herself had enrolled locally to take two 'A' levels: Art and English – the same subjects she'd given up in 1966.

She was about to meet Julian.

"Ready?" asked Michael.

"As ready as I'll ever be." Emma wasn't as nervous as she thought she'd be. She could relate to Julian's letters. She felt as if she loved him.

But what if he wasn't her son, if she'd found the wrong person? Would she know? Would she still feel as if she loved him? And what did he feel? Nothing? Curiosity? Anger?

"You're quiet," observed Michael.

"I just feel weird, I've waited so long and now it's happening."

"Well it won't be happening if you don't hurry up and get your coat on."

The pub was called The Three Cocks and was situated on a quiet country lane off the main Huntingdon Road. They had found it easily and were far too early.

"Might as well go in and have a drink," said Michael.

Emma sat in silence with her glass of bitter lemon. Michael threw light hearted chatter in her direction every few minutes, but got only polite nods and smiles in return.

Eight pm. Now Julian was late. Perhaps he wouldn't come. Perhaps he was here already and they hadn't recognized each other. Emma cast her eyes around the pub lounge. A young man stood at the bar with his wife chatting to the barman. Was that him? She tried to catch his eye, but if she did, nothing registered. Anyway, he was overweight and about thirty. Not Julian.

8.30. Michael was getting worried for her. Should he say anything?

Emma's eyes were on the door. "Here he is," she said breathlessly.

As soon as they walked in, she knew it was him. Thank God he'd come. She felt overwhelmed. Julian and Emma stared at each other. Michael stood up, shook his hand, held Becci's. They all smiled. Julian brought his eyes back to Emma. They acknowledged each other nervously. Emma half stood up to greet them, so overcome with emotion she felt disconnected, like a spectator.

"What'll it be?" asked Michael warmly.

"Oh, thanks. Er, a pint of lager, thanks – and you, Becci?" Julian seemed awkward, unsure. Beautiful.

185

"I'm glad you've come," Emma heard herself saying.

This is my son, she kept saying to herself. This man is my baby. The four of them exchanged small talk like guests at a dinner party. Photographs of Simon and Chloe were passed to them and they showed polite interest.

The only clue that this was no normal social meeting was the length of time Emma and Julian looked at each other. They were strangers – yet they felt some kind of link. It was more than curiosity. More than knowledge. For Emma at any rate, there was a physical pull. Every time Julian spoke, she was rivetted. His voice was already familiar from their brief telephone conversation and photographs had shown what he looked like, but this was a moving, warm, expressive face. He was alive, in the flesh.

Emma's previous sense of being in love was adapting to his presence; her maternal feelings of longing had found the object of her desire. She watched his mouth move as he spoke, the cute upward curve of his lips at the corners. His nose was straight. A good nose, not as small as hers but softer than John's. His eyes were the same rich brown as Emma's, yet piercing, intense, under strong expressive eyebrows that rose in animation, almost arrogantly, just the same as John's. A short, thick mop of blond hair, a square jaw, but not as heavy as his father's. He was a good-looking blend of the two of them, but taller and leaner than either John or her.

She wanted to touch him, smell him, feel the warmth of his skin, his breath on her face. He was a stranger. He was her son.

Time rolled back to the kitchen at Boulter Street as she recalled their last meeting. She had scooped the swaddled bundle from his cot and held him close to her. Just holding him there had made her breasts tingle. He had smelt sweet, a tiny drop of moisture glistened on his lips. Softly she had licked his mouth, then scattered his tiny face with kisses, burrowing into him, smothering his nose and cheeks with hers. Her nose had buried into his warmth and she had drawn his baby fragrance into her, his small breaths blanketed with hers…then they had come to take him away.

The door had closed.

Almost twenty-nine years later he was back, sitting opposite her around a pub table. Emma felt overloaded.

"I think, Julian," said Becci sweetly, looking at her watch, "it's time we made a move."

"Sure," agreed Julian. He nodded. He looked tired, drained. So was Emma. They were both exhausted. Michael smiled and said what a pleasure it had been meeting them, that maybe he and Emma could look forward to seeing them again shortly and that perhaps they would be interested in having a drink with Simon and Chloe sometime.

Slowly, all four of them got up and went into the car park. Julian politely ushered Becci and Emma in front of him, and Emma was acutely aware of his body just behind her. He was much taller than her, probably six foot compared to her five foot four. Michael shook Julian's hand and lightly brushed a kiss on Becci's cheek. Emma did likewise to Becci and turned to Julian.

He smiled and opened his arms. Emma laid herself into him and wrapped her arms around his body. They held each other silently for three or four minutes and she remembered her vow from many years ago. Love you, babe. I'll find you again one day. Promise. And she had. She had found him.

"Well what do you think? How do you reckon it went?" Michael was driving fast, full of adrenalin. But Emma said nothing. She tried to make some kind of comment, but her eyes were closed, her head tilted back, completely worn out. She could feel warm tears gently trickling down her cheeks and was vaguely aware that she wore a silly huge grin from ear to ear.

Reminders of Christmas had just been put on display at the supermarket. It seemed too soon. Late October. Emma didn't feel remotely "Christmassy". Yet for the first time since she was eighteen, the thought of November, dark cold nights, followed by December, Christmas trees and the sound of carols did not fill her with sadness. On the contrary. This year, Emma would be able to celebrate Christmas wholeheartedly. Simon and Chloe would be home for the winter holidays; it had already been tentatively arranged that all three of them – Simon, Chloe and Julian, with Becci, would meet for a drink. Julian and Becci might even stay with them for a few days depending on his family's commitments.

Emma pushed her shopping trolley through the aisles, selecting tins of this and packets of that, humming contentedly. Chloe was coming home for the weekend to hear all about her mum's reunion with Julian which meant soya mince and bean burgers. Emma wondered what food Julian liked, perhaps Indian or Italian? Did he take milk and sugar in his coffee? She wanted to know so much about him.

Emma paused in the babywear department. She and Michael had been to see George and Margaret last weekend and Margaret had lovingly shown her the baby's layette she had prepared for their forthcoming grandchild. Emma fingered a white baby-grow with a yellow bunny rabbit motif on the front. 0-3 months it said on the label. Oh how tiny! She had been bursting to tell them of her own imminent biological grandchild but George and Margaret knew nothing of Julian. Michael didn't want them to know. He still felt slightly uncomfortable sharing Emma's past himself, and Emma complied with his wishes.

She didn't want to. She wanted to shout about Julian's existence from the roof tops, but she didn't want Michael's disapproval again.

"You must tell Granddad!" Chloe sat on the floor, Sam flat on his back between her legs. She rubbed her hands all over his stomach much to Sam's approval.

"Oh Chloe...I don't know. We've never mentioned the baby since he was born. It's probably easier not to now, for his sake as much as anything. I'm not sure how he would handle it, or even if he'd want to."

Chloe didn't approve of secrets in the family. "Well did he ask about Granddad or Grandma?"

"No."

"Did he ask about me?" Chloe puckered her eyebrows.

"Not exactly, but Dad and I showed him photos of you and Simon. He was interested, sort of nodded and smiled."

"Is that all?"

"It isn't easy, Chloe. We kept the conversation very light."

Chloe stood up, a look of disappointment on her face. A full flop of mahogany fringe covered one eye. "Okay. So did you hug?" persisted Chloe.

"Yes."

"Good! How have Julian's parents been?"

Emma felt her body tense. "Er, I don't really know. We didn't talk about them."

"Lorraine once told me her mum and dad would go to pieces if she tried to find her birth mother. She said it would be like having an affair."

"Oh?" Emma felt uncomfortable. "I don't see how it can be like an affair."

"Well, in a way I can," Chloe ran her fingers through her fringe, flicking it back. "Like if Lorraine and her mum are so close, then one day, Lorraine said 'Oh by the way, Mum, meet my other mum' it would be like an affair. Like Dad coming home and suddenly wanting you to share him with another woman. Like you've been the one to wash his clothes, cook the dinner, do the shopping, cheer him up when he's down...and bang. He has another woman. Not instead of you, but as well as."

Emma frowned. "I don't think it's quite like that, love! I'm not in competition with Julian's mother. I might have given birth to him, but Mrs Brandon is Julian's mother."

"I wonder if she sees it that way, though. It would be good if you could talk to each other. It might make things easier for Julian."

"I don't think that it's possible at the moment."

"Can't you write to her?"

"Er, no... Well I did. Once. It wasn't very well received." Emma flushed. Even her own daughter could make her squirm.

"You did?" Chloe saw the pain in her mum's eyes. "God, why are people so anal?"

Emma wondered quite what "anal" meant, but decided not to ask.

November 24th. Julian's birthday.

He and Becci had accepted an invitation to stay the night following a celebratory meal. Four bottles of wine were in the fridge, although Emma drank considerably less these days. A large fresh chicken lay already quartered in the rack underneath and a selection of prepared vegetables stood in cold water.

In the living room were four parcels. The white baby-grow with the yellow bunny rabbit motif. A set of soaps and body lotion for Becci. Two birthday presents for Julian. Emma had agonized over what to buy him for his birthday. In the end she had bought him a small teddy bear – as a joke. And to acknowledge their mother and child relationship. In any event, he could give it to their baby. And, a Sekonda watch – to symbolize the passage of time. Leaning against the parcels was a birthday card, signed "With love from Emma, Michael, Simon and Chloe."

"Should I wear jeans or smarten up a bit, Michael?"

Michael looked up at his wife over his half moon glasses. He sat at the kitchen table with the crossword in front of him, pencil in hand. "You look fine," he smiled. "Stop flapping and relax."

"So when's the baby due, Becci?" asked Emma.

Becci was picking at her food. "January 18th," she smiled politely. She seemed uncomfortable and the atmosphere was tense.

"Looking forward to fatherhood Julian?" asked Michael.

Julian nodded, "I think so."

Emma stared at him, seeing John, seeing herself. The pull to touch him was stronger than ever. He wore khaki casual slacks, a biscuit coloured cotton shirt and an Arran sweater which he had taken off. She found herself wondering what he looked like naked.

"And your mother and father?" asked Michael topping up the wine glasses, "ready to be grandparents?" Emma thought this question rather brave, but welcomed it.

Julian sat upright and gave a quick sideways glance at Becci. "Er, yes. I...I think so."

"Do they know you're here tonight?" risked Emma.

A definite bristling from the pair of them.

"I er, I can't remember whether I mentioned it," muttered Julian.

Becci looked directly at Julian disapprovingly, then at Emma. "No. They don't know." Emma couldn't work out whether Becci's disapproval was directed at Julian or her but no more was said.

After their meal, the four of them retired into the living room and Emma gave Becci and Julian their presents. They were both delighted. Then they browsed through old photograph albums. Julian sat next to Emma and showed considerable interest in the photos, especially of Emma as a young girl at Boulter Street. He asked her about her childhood, her parents, her life in London and finally Simon and Chloe. Nothing personal or intrusive. At ten pm, Becci showed signs of tiredness and apologetically asked if she might go to bed.

"Of course," said Emma. Emma got up and led her to the spare bedroom. "If there's anything you want, just say. I'm sure Julian will be up soon."

At the bottom of the stairs, Michael stood alone. "Tell you what, I'll go too. Leave you both alone."

"Are you sure?"

Michael nodded, poked his head round the living room door and excused himself. Emma suddenly felt nervous yet exhilarated. A warmth flushed over her and she hoped her face wasn't red. She resumed her seat next to him on the settee.

Slowly, very slowly, they talked. Emma told him about John, of their youth in Newcastle, her pregnancy – even the big brown pills – of the birth, that he was born at 11.45, and she talked of her mum. Then she related the years that followed: London, drugs, New York and meeting Michael. Of her denial and shutting off, then about her mum's death, the newspaper announcement, the overwhelming sorrow and loss and obsessive search to find him. She had his hand in hers. He remained silent, listening.

"I'm sorry...about at first," he said uncomfortably. "You know, about not wanting to see you."

"That's okay. I guess I did it all wrong. It must have thrown you."

"Well, it wasn't just me. I haven't always done and said what I've wanted to."

"No?" Emma could feel the warmth of her son next to her.

"My parents have understandably been very shocked by your appearance." His voice had become correct, protective. "They think that any communication between the two of us should have been made through an official body."

"Probably. What about you? What do you think?"

"It's not really to do with what I think. I mean, I can see their point of view," Julian paused, "I love them very much, you know."

"Good. I'm pleased you do."

They were both silent for a moment before Emma continued. "Are you glad I found you?"

"Yes."

Julian seemed to feel a mixture of responsibility, concern, loyalty and loss. Emma still had his hand in hers, stroking his fingers. He gave nothing back, just let her hold his hand. They looked at each other and smiled. Slowly Emma slid her hand up the side of his face, soft bristles brushed lightly beneath her fingertips. Softly, tenderly, she stroked his hair and kissed him lightly on the cheek. Suddenly he was Oliver again. The warmth of his cheek under her lips, the soft smell of his skin and hair. Instinctively now, driven by maternal hunger, she stood up to face him, so that his head could be pressed into her body. She wrapped her arms around him, holding him tightly, then, still facing forwards, eased down onto her knees. He didn't move. He didn't stop her. Tenderly, she kissed his hair and caressed his face, totally immersed in a primal need for intimacy. Sensual waves inappropriately washed over them, yet it wasn't sexual. It made them feel close and it felt good. Neither of them knew how long they held each other. Neither of them realized it was two am. Neither of them knew how long Michael had been standing there in the doorway in his dressing gown.

Visibly shaken by their close embrace, Michael finally spoke. "What the hell are you two doing?"

Chapter Seventeen

Sam was ill. The old carcass of a long dead pigeon had proved indigestible even for his hardened stomach. He lay forlorn in his basket, ears down, with dull, sad eyes.

Jack was ill. The damp winter months had worsened his rheumatics, giving rise to fever and malaise.

Emma and Michael were having difficulties again. Their lack of communication was creating misunderstandings.

And it was Christmas. Chloe was home and Simon with his new girlfriend, Sara, would be arriving on the 23rd. Only a month ago, Emma had hoped it would be the family's best Christmas ever.

She hadn't heard from Julian since their last meeting a month ago. No phone call, no letter, not even a Christmas card. Emma had tried to ring him but it was always the answerphone. She'd sent a Christmas card and she'd written – but no reply. The last thing she wanted to do was hound him but the withdrawal was hurting her unbearably.

Chloe dunked a stick of celery into her cucumber and yoghurt dip while watching Emma iron. "Honestly Mum, you'd really like Martin. He's into sixties memorabilia – collects old Beatles records and pop art posters."

"Oh yes? And what about Stewart?"

Sam waddled pathetically to the kitchen door pausing briefly to sniff Chloe's nibbles. Emma and Chloe smiled at each other before Chloe slipped off the stool to open the door.

"If celery's turning him on, then he must be getting better," said Chloe. "Stewart? God he's so immature!"

Emma nodded without comment. She knew this was purely a time for listening, and it was a privilege that Chloe enjoyed sharing it with her.

Chloe fell silent for an unusual length of time, stirring her celery vigorously round the bowl of dip before looking back up at her mother. "I think I'd like to be with Martin when I meet Julian."

"Yes I'm sure that would be nice but I'm not sure how Julian is at the moment, er, over things."

"Why? What do you mean?"

Emma felt reluctant to talk, "I haven't heard from him since I saw him last."

"Oh Mum! That's less than a month ago! You sometimes don't hear from Simon much more often than that!"

Emma sighed, recalling now that intensity of feeling, her overwhelming flood of love for her son, Michael standing in the doorway confused, alarmed, Julian pulling away, a sleepless night and Becci's hostility the next morning. They had left early. Even to this day, she and Michael hadn't said a word about that night. He felt angry and excluded. He felt he'd made a supreme effort to be understanding, and still he was cut out. Emma was swamped with guilt, scared of loss, trapped by feelings she didn't want and at the mercy of emotions out of her control.

"I know, but it isn't easy. Maybe he's found out as much as he wants."

"You've only met him twice! And what about me? Doesn't he want to meet me?" Chloe sucked pensively on her celery and gazed at her mother through thickened lashes. She noticed her mum's eyes watering. "Oh Mum – what happened ?"

Emma found herself telling her daughter a large portion of the truth, watching constantly for signs of disapproval. There were none.

"Of course you love him, you're his mum! It's only natural you should want to bond, there's nothing wrong in that."

"I know but he's still a stranger, love. And a large handsome one at that. You can understand how your dad would have seen it."

"Honestly, you two are so anal. You need to talk! And so does Julian!" Chloe paused. "If his mother is against you meeting, and now Becci too – well who on earth will Julian talk to? Oh, the poor guy. And it must feel like shit to have been abandoned by your mum."

"I don't know about 'poor guy'," said Emma, "he's an adult man now. And I didn't abandon him, it's the way it was in those days."

"It's still abandoning, Mum. I'd hate to think you could have done that to me."

They sat in silence for a while. Perhaps it did feel like abandonment to Julian. However much Emma mourned, she had to face the fact that she'd had more control of his destiny than he'd had. And who could Julian talk to? Maybe it would be easier for him to forget her and stay within the safety of his own family. She was being selfish, trying to ease her own loss at everyone else's expense.

"Perhaps you just need some gap time," said Chloe. "I'll maybe phone him over Christmas when Simon's here. Nothing heavy. Just drag him out for a pint."

But that was not to be.

Jack was admitted to hospital on 24th December and died on Christmas Day. Last minute urgent journeys to Newcastle and back – and to Newcastle again, combined with Christmas preparations that came to nothing, a full house with Simon, Sara and Chloe, a cool detachment from Michael and hurt over Julian's withdrawal plus now the sadness of losing her father, had left Emma feeling overwhelmed. She was determined not to visit her doctor despite a recurrence of headaches and indigestion.

The funeral was the following Thursday. Emma would make the journey to Newcastle first, clear out some paperwork and make a start on the house. Michael, Simon, Sara and Chloe would arrive later that week. Steven, now separated from his wife, would be staying for a few days to attend his father's funeral and lend a hand before returning to Canada.

As she was packing a small suitcase in the bedroom, Emma froze. She was catapulted back with absolute clarity: Sheena, cannabis, the double bedsit in Brunswick Gardens…she could almost smell the pot, feel them both swaying in a drug-induced euphoria. Chloe was playing *We Can Work it Out* on her CD player.

Emma stood there transfixed. She had always loved this song, loved the words, it had always made her believe everything would be fine. A tender recollection of that unstable and disturbed eighteen-year-old tore at Emma's heart. What a wreck I was.

Can we work it out? she thought.

May 8th. The sun shone and an early summer warmth had persuaded Emma to dig out a thin cotton skirt she'd bought last summer in Florida only to find it hanging loosely on her. She must have lost over a stone in weight during the last year.

Lorraine nibbled her bottom lip and puckered her eyebrows whilst grooming a recently spayed cat. "Five months? Well, maybe he just needs a breather for a while. I'm sure he'll be in touch again when he's ready."

"Do you think so, Lorraine? Oh I don't know, I just wish I knew what he was feeling. Perhaps I should let go of it – but I feel all in limbo somehow." Emma was a mess. There was the counsellor Amanda, but she didn't want to see her again. Lorraine was now looking for her birth parents. But it was perhaps unfair to share her anguish with her.

"What about the father? You could get in touch with him and talk to him about it."

"John? Oh I don't know about that. Not behind Michael's back, not after how good he's been."

"No, not behind his back. I didn't mean that. Tell Michael of course, but share it with John – after all, he's the father."

Emma pulled a face. "Er, Michael wouldn't like me to get in touch with John."

"Why not? Julian was born years ago! It's hardly an ongoing affair. Couples these days often have a child from a past relationship. It could be healthier for all of you." Lorraine caressed the cat more softly now. "I mean, it takes a lot of guts you know."

"Guts? Who for – me?"

"No…well, yes of course. But Julian. I mean, maybe he's feeling mixed up. He's probably just trying to keep everyone else happy. There are a lot of risks involved for him, like who's on *his* side?" Lorraine placed the cat in its basket ready for the owners to collect it.

"If I try to get in touch with him again it will be harassment. Maybe his family are giving him a hard time too. Oh dear. I see what you mean."

Lorraine shrugged her shoulders helplessly. She looked lost.

When Emma phoned John the following week, his landlady informed her he'd moved to Australia. No forwarding address. He'd gone. Just like that. Perhaps just as well.

The new owners of 37 Boulter Street wanted to move in on August 15th. The sale had been quite straightforward and in due course, Emma and Steven would inherit a substantial amount of money. She had hoped closing the door on that house for the very last time would close an era. But the sense of loss still dragged with her like an arthritic limb.

It seemed to Emma that for everyone else Julian's existence was receding into the past. Life had quite simply picked up the pieces and carried on. Chloe had dropped mention of him. Simon had gained a 2:1 in Industrial Design, found work in a studio in Brighton and planned to marry Sara within a couple of years. He had never really mentioned Julian and Emma would now never know his feelings.

Chloe had completed her one year foundation art course and now, still in Loughborough and living with Martin, was training as a photo-journalist with a local free newspaper. Emma herself was planning in time to take an Open University degree course.

The summer was unusually hot and dry. It was the first summer Michael and Emma had spent alone without family. They enjoyed leisurely sunset walks with Sam, weekends gardening, barbeques with George and Margaret, and their children's frequent visits with and without partners.

Julian never made contact again. Nor was he ever mentioned. And although a sadness and confusion lay within Emma, as the cool, darker nights approached, it no longer hurt all the time. If anything, she was just glad she had at least met him, hugged him. It gave her a huge sense of release and relief – and though she had so wanted Julian to be a constant link, maybe it was not meant to be. And she felt closer to Michael and all her family. All she really hoped for, prayed for, was that Julian was happy.

As the acute sense of loss faded a little, she grew more relaxed in herself. No complicated internal or emotional knots, or blocks. And no more migraines, indigestion, or anxiety.

"Dad," Chloe was curled on the settee, swigging lager from a bottle. Sam lay at her feet. Emma didn't allow him in the living room but she was away for the weekend on an Aromatherapy course with Margaret.

"Mmm?" Michael continued reading his novel.

"You know Julian?"

He gently lay the book in his lap and looked at Chloe, "Yes?"

"What happened? Why didn't you and Mum see him again?"

Although the subject was a surprise, Michael was quite relaxed talking to Chloe about Julian. In fact he almost welcomed it. With Emma, it was still too sensitive. "I think it was probably too much for him to handle. Your mother was quite obsessed over him and it probably unnerved him."

Chloe frowned. "Does that mean that's it?"

"Oh I don't know, love. Remember he was busy with his career, newly married with a mortgage and a baby on the way."

Chloe rubbed her feet in her woolly socks over Sam's back. He groaned in pleasure. "What about me? Wouldn't he want to see me?"

"Well, I'm afraid if Julian doesn't want to get in touch, that really has to be the way it is. He must be allowed to make his own choices without pressure, especially from us."

"I don't mean pressure, but more reassurance."

"I think that might come over as even greater pressure. Your mother has done more than enough to show her feelings." Michael recalled Emma's and Julian's embrace. What no-one realized was how he felt he understood their feelings. At thirty-two, his own mother had died after years of estrangement. He'd felt lost and had secretly cried, desperate for her love. Not that he'd been adopted, he didn't know what that felt like, but he understood the childish need for parental affection even in adulthood. He knew the need for love was quite scary, not that he and Emma had ever talked about it.

"What about you, Dad?"

"Me? It's got nothing to do with me, has it?"

"Of course it has! How do you feel about Julian?"

So someone had asked him. For the first time, someone had actually asked him. How nice. Michael smiled warmly. "I admit it was a shock that wobbled us, but I'm far more sympathetic than your mother realizes. I think her guilt has stopped her seeing that."

Chloe stared hard into her bottle. "That's not what I asked. I asked you how you felt about Julian."

"Ha! Well you have put me a spot," he smiled, almost embarrassed. "If I'm to be honest, I know it seems strange...but in a way," Michael cleared his throat, "I feel, um, quite fond of him."

"So do I, Dad. And so does Simon."

Michael raised his eyebrows. The mention of his son's name in relation to this was quite interesting. He had often wondered about Simon's reaction but had never asked.

"Well, what if he's got stuck..." continued Chloe, "like supposing at first he needed loads of space to get his head round things – but now daren't make a move in case he gets rejected. And even if he doesn't want to meet us, it would be kind of reassuring for him to know we care anyway. It could be you're just the right one to make contact."

"Oh I think it would be wrong of me to do anything without your mother's say so. He's had enough opportunities, believe me."

"But he might be testing her or even trying to hurt her. Just checking out that however much he snubs her, or us, Mum will still be there for him. That she will never reject him again, however bad he is or however horrible he is."

"That sounds a bit heavy, Chloe. I think perhaps you've read too many sociology text books."

Chloe looked deadly serious and shook her head assertively. "How does Mum feel?"

"Er, well, I don't know, we don't really talk about it." Michael knew what was coming. Chloe plonked her bottle down on the table disapprovingly and a small froth of beer fell onto Sam's back.

"You don't talk about it?"

"It only causes upset, and she seems so much better these days it's probably best left alone. Even your mother might now prefer not to renew contact."

"Bullshit. She's just resigned to getting on with life. She's more realistic now, lower expectations. Anyway, what about Julian? And what about me?

How do you think I feel? I think about him all the time. I mean, what's it been now? Months – years! He's my brother and I've never met him. It won't go away..." Chloe opened her arms, "by ignoring it."

"He may not want any further contact, Chloe. You have to understand and respect that other people are not necessarily as open as you."

Chloe shook her head. "We need to throw a line out. Not tell Mum, because if he doesn't bite then she doesn't need to know. It will be better coming from you so he knows you're behind her and you're okay about everything. We must make sure he knows we still want him. And always will."

Michael frowned. "Again?"

"Yep. Again and again and again."

"Isn't that rather intrusive?"

"Not as long as it's offered freely without obligation. And..." continued Chloe authoritatively, "you should book yourself and Mum a decent holiday. Have a second honeymoon – well, a first really, 'cos you never had a proper one, did you? Why not whizz off somewhere tropical?"

"Maybe sometime."

"'Maybe sometime' what? Julian or holiday?"

"Oh I don't know!" Michael laughed at Chloe's persistence. Thank goodness she was only home for a weekend. "Maybe both, okay?"

Chloe sniffed, and winked at him. "Promise?"

"Oh Chloe. Yes. Okay."

Michael was alone. Emma was at Sainsbury's. He held the phone in his hand, heart thumping, and tapped out the digits. Someone the other end picked up the receiver.

"Hello?"

This is stupid, he thought, yet his throat felt so dry he had to push the words out. "Hello, is Julian there please?"

"Speaking. Who's that?"

"It's er – Michael, Emma's husband."

Part Four

Chapter Eighteen

Emma twisted round in the dress cubicle, craning her neck to examine bits of her rarely seen in the reflection of mirrors. Whoops Those extra pounds were creeping on again. Ah well. Not to worry. She scooped up her long hair on top of her head, pouted her lips sexily and sucked her tummy in before she recklessly decided on both dresses. The green and the russet. After all, one didn't have a twenty-fifth wedding anniversary celebration every day, and this way she could take her time in making up her mind which one to wear. She paid for the goods and looked at her watch: 12.15. Emma had arranged to meet Margaret for lunch at the Wine Cellar at 12.30, so swiftly gathering her bag of clothes, she swung into the High Street, through the market and into the little cobbled alleyway where Margaret was already waiting.

In the pub, dim lights and dark, intimate decor made an unwelcome contrast to the sun outside; the delicious smell of food reminded Emma how hungry she was.

"It's not as if I've ever said a thing," moaned Margaret twiddling with the stem of her wine glass. "Reuben is as mad with her as we are, but she insists we've alienated her and their child. And Ireland is so far away. I don't know when we'll see our granddaughter again."

"Oh you poor thing," said Emma as a waitress brought their meals to the table, "But maybe Beth and Reuben will want to make another go of things? They only split up last month."

"I don't think so. I think their marriage is over. Of course I always told Reuben he was too young, but you know how it is. Always think they know better. And these days couples walk out on each other at the first hint of trouble." Margaret sighed deeply and cast her eyes down onto her plate of ham salad. "Not like George and me – we worked things out."

George's infidelity still shocked Emma, although Michael had since confided to her that he had often "had a bit on the side" as he'd put it. Not that she'd said anything to Margaret, of course.

"How are things now?" asked Emma.

"Oh I don't know. One minute I can handle it and the next it slaps me right in the face again. She is such a bloody tart! I just don't know how he could." Margaret pushed her untouched food away.

"It was only a whim, Margaret. Male menopause – don't let it destroy all you've got between you."

"Was it?" Margaret rolled her eyes up to the ceiling before looking hard at Emma. "How can I believe anything now?"

They remained silent for a while, Margaret sipping her wine, Emma delving hungrily into her lasagne.

"You know you're very lucky with Simon and Chloe," said Margaret eventually. "They're doing so well, both in their careers and with good stable relationships."

Emma laughed and paused from her meal to take a sip of mineral water. "So far, but it's only August. Could all be a different story by the end of the year!"

It wasn't just Emma's children that Margaret was envious of, but her long red hair, her bright amber eyes, her confidence and sense of fun. And her marriage. "So what did you buy then?" she asked, changing the subject.

Emma lay the knife and fork down on her empty plate, moved it slightly to one side and lifted up the carrier bag. "I've bought two dresses, Margaret; Michael will despair! But honestly, I just couldn't make up my mind which one! And I'm getting so fat again I'll probably need a third by September!"

"Oh Emma, you aren't fat. I like the russet dress," said Margaret handling the edge of its hem. She looked at Emma seriously now and lowered her voice, "You know not so long ago, I never thought you and Michael would be together to share your twenty-fifth."

Emma grinned, almost sheepishly. She had once felt so drab and pathetic next to Margaret, jealous of what she considered her and George's electric sexual connection. Now it was Margaret who seemed vulnerable and tired.

"Anyway, ready for your celebrations?"

"I think so. The room's booked, the catering organized, the invitations all sent out."

"*Everyone* coming?"

The shopping list was so crumpled and dog-eared Emma could hardly read her own handwriting. Dress. Sandals. Sun-tan cream. Mushrooms. Lunch with Margaret. Writing paper & envelopes. Travel agents. Look at wedding dresses. Mmm. What next? Maybe the travel agents, just pop in to book the travellers cheques and currency and confirm the tickets will be ready within a couple of weeks. Their silver wedding was on the last Saturday in September. A private party was being held in one of the rooms at the golf club, and – unbeknown to anyone save her, Michael, George and Margaret, they were leaving at 9.30pm for what they were calling their second honeymoon. In actual fact, they had already enjoyed a couple of very happy holidays abroad recently, but this one was a little further afield.

Emma's packages were multiplying. The list had only got "Look at wedding dresses" left on it. She debated whether to forget that and go straight home as her arms were aching, but decided on a brief wander around Debenham's bridal department. Chloe wouldn't have approved but never mind. Emma knew Chloe would marry Martin one day and, she suspected, it would be a conventional wedding. After all, remember the nose rings? The dyed hair? The clothes? And now look at her. Twenty-four, smart, a successful photo-journalist with a growing list of private functions to attend to.

"Emma…" a tap on the shoulder jolted her round.

She was so surprised at the price of a plain silk gown that at first the sound of her own name didn't register. "Oh goodness! Lorraine!"

For a few moments the two of them stood facing each other with broad grins across their faces. Lorraine had left the veterinary practice two years ago. They hadn't managed to keep in touch. An older woman, probably about the same age as Emma, was with her.

"It's great to see you!" Emma nodded towards the silk bridal gown, " you're not…?"

"Actually, yes." grinned Lorraine sheepishly. Then she turned to the lady she was with. "Jean, this is Emma. She works as a receptionist at Mr Crossley's practice. Emma, this is Jean – my mum."

Jean held out a hand and shook Emma's warmly.

"So you've got an expensive time ahead of you then?" smiled Emma letting her eyes skim the shop floor.

"Well, perhaps not me so much," Jean flushed uncomfortably.

"Jean's my birth mum," explained Lorraine hurriedly.

"Oh..."

"I found her. It's great, isn't it?" she asked, looking at Jean.

Emma stared back at Jean and realized her mouth was open. Emma felt flooded with – what? Compassion? Empathy? She found herself saying hello, which was silly because they'd already said hello.

"It's been wonderful," continued Lorraine happily, "honestly since then, so much has happened... I met Rob. He's great! You know I moved to The Circle Veterinary Practice, well he came in one day with his dobermann and we just clicked! I'm senior vet nurse now. It's really nice there, the girls are smashing." Lorraine paused momentarily for breath. "How's Chloe?"

"Fine, fine," said Emma, Lorraine's rushed chatter spinning in her ears. She wanted to hug Jean. "She's still with Martin."

"And Simon? Michael?"

"Great, yes they're fine."

Lorraine paused. "And Julian?"

Emma rolled her eyes. It was an inevitable question. She looked at Jean first, then Lorraine before taking a deep breath. Would this ever be easy? "Well, I met him. But then..."

The meeting left Emma disorientated. She was delighted to see Lorraine after all this time, but it had bothered her meeting Jean. Still, everything was fine now. She remembered her counselling sessions with Amanda. Goodness, how distraught she'd been then! Emma shook her head and tut-tutted aloud. Amanda. Emma walked through the store and out onto the busy High Street. "I wonder if she's still there?" thought Emma.

"Do you have an appointment?" asked a smiling receptionist.

" o. I was just passing and wondered if Amanda still worked here."

" es she does, but I don't think she's in today. If you'd just like to wait a moment I'll buzz her office." The receptionist turned herself and the telephone receiver away from Emma and tapped in some digits. She turned back. " ou're in luck. She's on her way down."

"Emma!" Amanda opened her arms. They hugged briefly. "Shall we get some tea? Oh this is wonderful to see you! I've often thought about you." Emma followed as Amanda breezed towards a counselling room. She felt how she'd felt when she followed Sheena through Miss Selfridge on her first day of work there.

"Well, how are you?" beamed Amanda.

Emma sat on the same chair, cup of tea in her lap. A box of toys stood in the corner. She momentarily regretted coming. "I'm great," grinned Emma. " eally good."

Amanda nodded approvingly, remaining silent.

"It's our silver wedding anniversary next month," said Emma, continuing happily with a brief resume of the family's news to date. Then she took a sip of tea and gently replaced the cup onto its saucer before looking into Amanda's eyes. Deep breath. "I met him…"

" ow was it?"

Emma placed the cup and saucer on the floor and ran her hands through her hair. "Oh I don't know. Well I do. It was okay – at first." Amanda encouraged Emma to continue. "I mean, like he was a stranger, yet physically – for me anyway – there was a bond. It's hard to describe. et as I say, I didn't know him."

"Oh?"

" erhaps this happens? First you fall in love with them and feel euphoric. Then you hunger after them and it's obsessive. Then you find them – but it's not what you've been looking for. The dream and reality are poles apart. And then, finally, if you're lucky, you start to build on solid foundations – warts an' all, until you're left with – well, whatever you're left with."

"And where are you now?"

"I guess the emotional turmoil has burnt itself out," Emma shrugged her shoulders and raised her eyebrows. ad it? Then she shuffled uncom - fortably on her seat and looked at Amanda, wondering how much she dare tell her. " ut at first I really had a job with my emotions. e needed space. I had to let go."

Amanda smiled and nodded.

Four bags of shopping lay on the floor. Emma realized she must get home. She'd been so busy chattering away, she'd not got around to telling Amanda the most important news.

" ave you got another ten minutes?" Amanda nodded. "That's not the end of the story."

Chapter Nineteen

"Katy Katy Katy!" shrieked Emma. Sam lifted an anxious head from his basket, unnerved by the outburst. Emma started jumping up and down on the spot, the telephone receiver bouncing with her.

Michael heard her scream and rushed into the kitchen, stepping over suitcases as he did so, but a beaming Emma waved her arm to indicate excited good news.

"When?" More jumping up and down on the spot. "Oh wow! WOW! I am happy for you."

Michael listened, unable to work it out. Sam closed his eyes.

"Are you? That'll wear off soon. When's it due? Oh wow! It'll be Pisces!" Emma peeled herself away from the mouthpiece, "Katy's expecting a baby, Michael – isn't that wonderful!"

Michael nodded but was rather confused. Wasn't she infertile? Wasn't she forty-something? Wasn't she single? Oh well, it obviously appeared to be good news. Women had some strange ideas about having babies. He picked up the bag with Sam's blanket, collected his lead and walked up to the dog.

"Come on Sam. Kennels I'm afraid. We are going to a party – and then on holiday."

Just at that moment, Chloe arrived. "Hiya!" she beamed entering the kitchen, Martin just behind her. "Oh Sammy Wammy baby…is Daddy taking you to those horrible kennels, my little one?" Chloe fell onto the floor, dropping bags behind her, to collapse over Sam's aging body. After several kisses, Chloe's prostrate body twisted to see why her mother sounded so overjoyed. They exchanged waves and slowly, she stood up, dusted herself down and flung her arms around Michael.

"Bye then Katy!" Emma mouthed hello to her daughter. "Of course I will. As soon as we get there. You get those feet up. Yes, yes I will. And you too. I'm so happy. Yes, I'll give them your love. About six-ish. No, just a buffet... Mmm, I hope so. He said he would. I know...ah, that's a secret! No. Not America. Will do. You too. Take care! Bye."

Emma turned to face her daughter and Martin. Chloe rushed to give her mum a big hug.

"Let's get that kettle on. That was Katy – in Florida. She's expecting a baby!"

"I'm just taking Sam to the kennels," said Michael.

"Okay love. Let's give him one last kiss – come here Sam. What's Daddy going to do to you then, my baby?" Emma fondled him and let him go back to Michael before turning her attention to Martin. "Hello Martin, how are you?"

"Fine thanks."

"A baby? Isn't she infertile?" asked Chloe, picking grapes off a fresh bunch. Emma was about to tell her not to, then remembered they were locking up the house and leaving it for three weeks in a few hours. Grapes and all.

"Yes, it's amazing! Isn't it wonderful!"

Chloe felt confused.

"Hiya Dad!" Simon met his father in the hall, his entrance having gone unnoticed amid the commotion. He squeezed into the kitchen.

"Bloody hell, off to Vladivostok or something?" Sara smiled beside him.

"Hi everyone," she said.

"I'm off to the kennels," said Michael.

"Oh dear. Not in the dog house again, are you?" quipped Simon.

Everyone groaned.

"Ha ha," grinned Michael sarcastically.

"Poor Sam," he continued, "are you going to the kennels and missing the party, poor thing." Sam's bottom was now wiggling side to side at the mass of family love in the kitchen. He so desperately wanted to stay, all these lovely voices, all this wonderful attention.

"Come on Sam," said Michael. "Let's go." And he left, glad to get away from the chaos.

"What are you going to wear, Mum?"

"Well, I need your help really, Chloe. I don't know whether to wear green or russet."

"Where are you going?" Chloe looked at the suitcases.

"Oh I don't know, love," lied Emma. "Wales probably."

The thought of Wales threw Chloe and Simon into deep comradeship. Yuk. Family memories in Wales. In polite disapproval they slid their attention back to their respective partners.

The party room had been secretly decorated by several members of the golf club under the enthusiastic supervision of George and Margaret. Silver balloons were pinned around the walls, a banner hung between two corners of the ceiling:

CONGRATULATIONS TO EMMA AND MICHAEL ON THEIR
SILVER WEDDING ANNIVERSARY

Along the length of the room, a table adorned with fresh flowers in little silver goblets boasted a delicious selection of sandwiches, cold meats, snacks and cheeses.

By the time Michael and Emma arrived, the room was full. Emma was nervous. Perhaps it was being the centre of attention; maybe it was the thought of their holiday; most likely it was the thought of seeing him again. It still excited her.

"Mum, you look gorgeous!" Chloe hugged her mum as if it had been considerably longer than an hour since she'd last seen her. Chloe was hugging everyone.

"Emma! Michael! Drink?"

"Thanks George," smiled Michael. "Just half a lager, I think."

"Emma?"

Emma scanned the room. There were friends from the golf club, a couple of Michael's colleagues and nurses from Emma's work. Lorraine and her fiancé. Oh wonderful! Emma waved. Then there was Margaret of course, and a cousin with her husband from Southampton. Huddled in a

corner at the far end were Martin, Sara and Simon – was it Simon? No…
No it wasn't! Emma's heart did a quick flip. Honestly, you could hardly tell
them apart from the back. No, there was Simon with Chloe talking to
Lorraine. Emma smiled broadly at George, so relieved. So happy. Perfect.

"Sorry George, I was just looking around. You've done a lovely job,"
Emma looked up at the decorations. "Just a water for me, thanks."

Emma noticed Chloe and Simon had joined the others in the corner.
They were laughing. Julian pulled Chloe's hair and she watched her
daughter punch him playfully in the stomach. Simon and Martin appeared
to join in and a mock argument ensued, causing more laughter.

"Emma. This is Rob."

"Hello Rob." Emma shook his hand. Lorraine sidled up to Emma and
whispered in her ear. "Where is he?"

"In the corner with the others." Emma winked. "You'll have to work out
who's who. I have a job myself!"

Lorraine squinted inquisitively and Emma hesitated, wondering
whether to ask about Jean but decided against it.

Michael was talking to the Southampton cousin's husband, Alan, and
George about the Internet.

"Quite honestly, it's all beyond me," said George. "It's the young ones
who're really up front with all this modern technology."

"The thing is," said Alan, "if you don't keep up, you lose out. Business is
being sought and found on the web."

"I'll tell you who's really the one to ask about this. My stepson; he
designs web sites."

Emma was barely in earshot and still talking to Lorraine and Rob
about their forthcoming wedding, but Michael's use of the word stepson
shot at her.

"Julian…!" Michael waved his arm. "He's the one." Julian walked up to
Michael politely, holding Bethany's hand. "This is Julian," said Michael,
"and his daughter, Beth."

George and Alan nodded. "Know about the Internet, do you?"

Julian's move, breaking up the younger group, prompted a mass surge
towards the food. Emma found herself standing next to Becci, once again
heavily pregnant.

"Not long now," said Emma.

"Thank goodness!"

"Becci's invited me to be Godmother," chirped Chloe, squeezing in at the table. "Oh oh. Here come the boys."

Simon, Martin and Julian leaned over them to reach the chunky ham sandwiches. Emma grinned at Julian and ducked under him to make room at the table. "You okay?" she asked.

"Sure," he smiled. "And you?"

"Yes."

"Congratulations."

"Sorry?"

"Silver wedding."

"Of course! Thanks." Recently, he'd met John, his birth father. She wanted to know how that had gone. Maybe Chloe or Simon would tell her in time, he seemed to share more with them. He was particularly close to Simon.

"Going to bloody Wales after this, you know," interrupted Simon squeezing in between them. "Some great holiday, eh?"

"Wales?" Michael now joined them.

"Yeah, Mum says you're both off to Wales."

Michael laughed. Emma watched him ruffle Simon's hair. "Wales eh?" Michael turned to Emma, "and to think we've had anti-malaria pills for Snowdonia!"

Chloe puckered her eyebrows and stared at them, but Margaret appeared and changed the subject. Sometimes Emma wondered what had happened to Julian to make him get in touch again. He had telephoned out of the blue and invited her and Michael round for a meal. Following that, a new relationship had started to evolve between Julian and herself. In some ways, she'd had to wade through certain disappointments, a recognition of irritating and unlikeable character traits in Julian had merged with an indestructible love for him. He seemed a little lazy and emotionally detached – not just from her, but in general. Also he slouched and often neglected his appearance, especially his hair. At one meeting they'd had a few months ago, she had told him to stand up straight. She apologized immediately, but he'd glared at her in confusion and shock. And then he'd stood up straighter.

He had also found disappointments in Emma. Although not as highly strung as she had once been, she was still inclined to be emotionally unpredictable. And Julian hated red hair. He didn't love Emma, even now, and he was always wary of her past heartache. It unnerved him. She was important to him and he'd also found a strong sense of identity in having this new family in addition to his real, adoptive parents. Genuine blood ties to his own biological past. And he liked Michael enormously.

Chloe wormed her way towards her mother, intent to work out the mysterious holiday destination, when a loud banging startled everyone into silence.

"Excuse me! Excuse me!" George was hammering on the table. The room gradually became still and quiet as faces turned towards him. "Ahem! Well now ladies and gentlemen, I think that I, on behalf of everyone here I'm sure, would like to make a toast to our very special couple this afternoon – Emma and Michael!" Everyone clapped, a few deep cheers rumbled through the room.

"Unaccustomed as I am to making speeches..." laughter rippled somewhere at the back, "I would just like to say that it is with very great pleasure Margaret and I congratulate our close friends with having made it to the twenty-five year marker! And I know I speak for all of us here when I say that such a celebratory union couldn't happen to a nicer couple. Like all of us who have weathered a few years, life has given both Emma and Michael their ups and downs, yet here they are now – reaping the rewards of half a lifetime's devotion." A few people clapped, someone laughed and suggested "perseverance".

George grinned good humouredly and continued, "I suggest we raise our glasses and toast this lovely couple on their silver wedding anniversary and wish them all the happiness they deserve for the next twenty-five years!"

"Here! Here!" shouted a male voice.

"Congratulations!" echoed Lorraine.

Everyone raised their glasses, chanting congratulations, followed by Simon calling. "Speech! Speech!" Michael pulled a face but the request ran through the crowd. Slowly, he placed his glass down on the table and faced all eyes in the room. His manner was confident, relaxed and happy. Emma watched him, she felt slightly embarrassed, yet proud. He thanked friends and family for their gifts, followed with loving yet humourous references to Simon, Chloe and Emma.

"…and finally, I would just like to add that without Emma, I would have nothing. I love her more than she knows, and I trust she will continue to put up with me for as long as forever is."

Chloe clapped the loudest and rushed up to hug both her mother and her father. Everyone started talking at once, Chloe had to almost shout to be heard. "But *where?*" she insisted.

Emma slipped her arm into Michael's and looked up at him. "Do you think we ought to leave soon?"

"Where are you really going?" Chloe, Simon, Julian, Martin, Sara, Becci and little Bethany waited expectantly.

"Well, you always said I should take your mother on a second honeymoon, somewhere tropical – so Tanzania," said Michael.

"Tanzania? When?" spluttered a chorus of offspring.

Michael looked at his watch just as George reappeared.

"Haven't you two got a plane to catch?"

Emma grinned at Chloe. "We're flying to Dar es Salaam late tonight. Then we're going on a ten day safari round the Ngorongoro crater and Serengeti followed with eight days in a luxury hotel in Zanzibar."

Six mouths hung open.

"Will you be all right, Mum?" asked Simon.

Emma's gaze fell briefly on Julian before answering. "Yes, just fine."

Margaret joined George with the family group. Only George and Margaret had known of their plans.

"Come on, team," urged George. "Shall we sneak you out?"

Chloe slipped an arm round each of her two brothers. "I'm really pleased for you. I really am." Chloe paused a moment before suddenly flashing enthusiastically, "Hey Dad! Mum! You know next year, can we all go somewhere together? All eight of us – and the kids?"

Michael recoiled in mock horror.

"Please…say yes! Even a cottage in Wales! It would be so special for us all to get together!"

"Oh Chloe," interrupted Emma awkwardly, "I don't think Julian and Becci would…"

"No, that sounds good, " smiled Julian.

Becci smiled and scooped up their daughter, resting her on the side of her hip. Simon grinned and looked at Sara. He didn't like to suggest it could be three children. After all, they weren't sure yet and not being married, he wasn't too sure how well received the news might be.

"C'mon!" George sounded worried, "you've got to get to Heathrow yet!"

It was time to go. Michael hugged Chloe and patted the arms of Simon and Julian, and kissed Bethany's cheek. Emma brushed hurried and unobtrusive lips on each and every one of them; she wanted to hug each one tightly but their exit was to be discreet.

George led the way and Michael took Emma's hand as they walked towards the fire exit out the back of the building. Out in the street, the air seemed cool and quiet. Escape. George waved, Margaret stood just behind him. Quickly Michael and Emma slid into their car. Their luggage was already packed in the boot.

At first they remained silent as if their elopment had to be conducted without communication, but once away from the golf club and out onto the open road, Michael started to laugh.

Emma looked at him. "What are you laughing at?"

"Bloody kids! That would make ten of us!"

Emma screwed her face up in concentration, tapping the fingers on her left hand with her right forefinger, muttering names softly under her breath. "Oh dear, yes…"

But still Michael laughed. A deep, rolling, contented laugh. It seemed infectious and Emma caught it too, though neither quite knew what they were laughing at. She rested her hand lightly on Michael's thigh and beamed.